Illuminate

Angie's Extreme Stress Menders
Volume 5

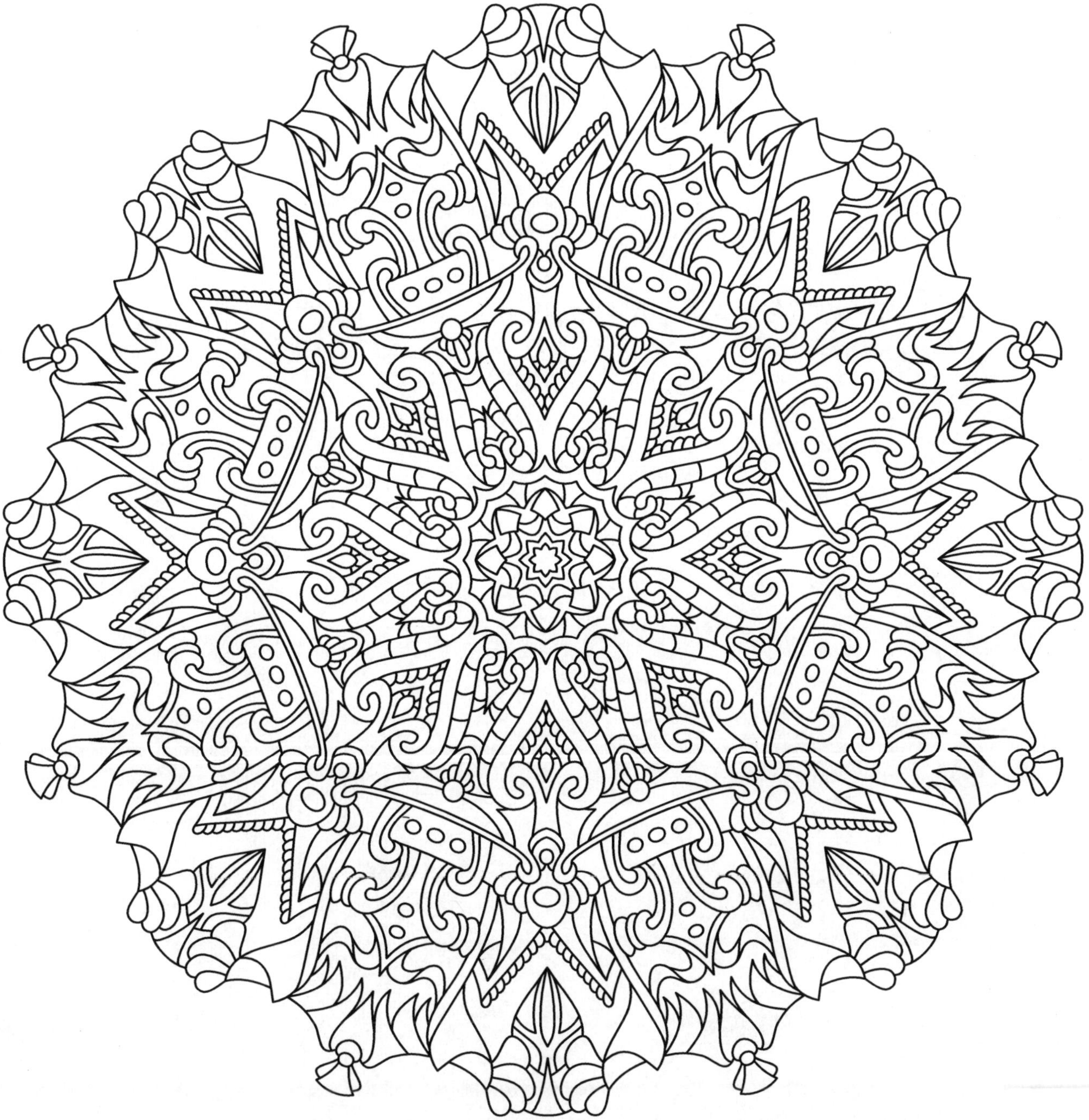

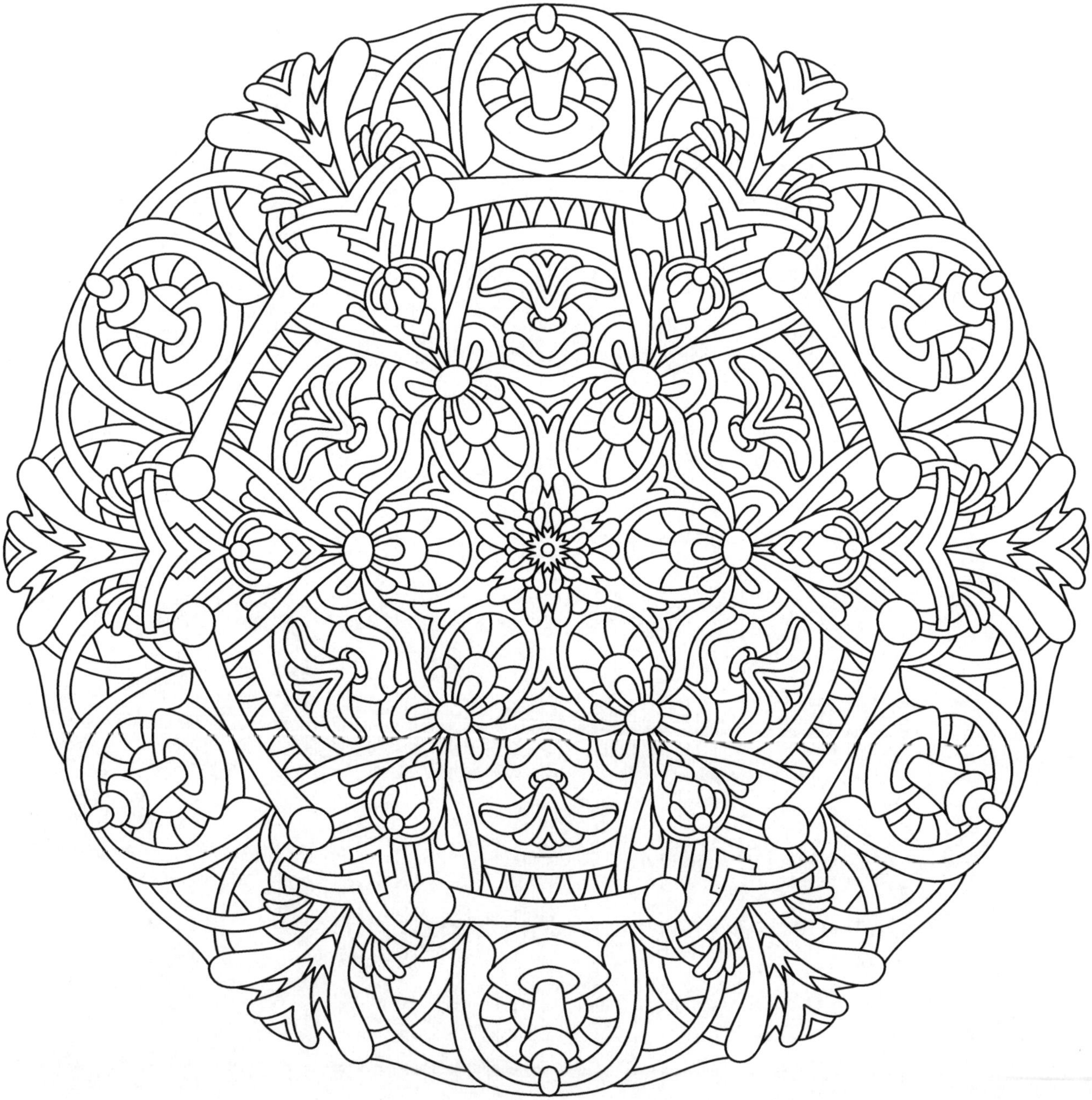

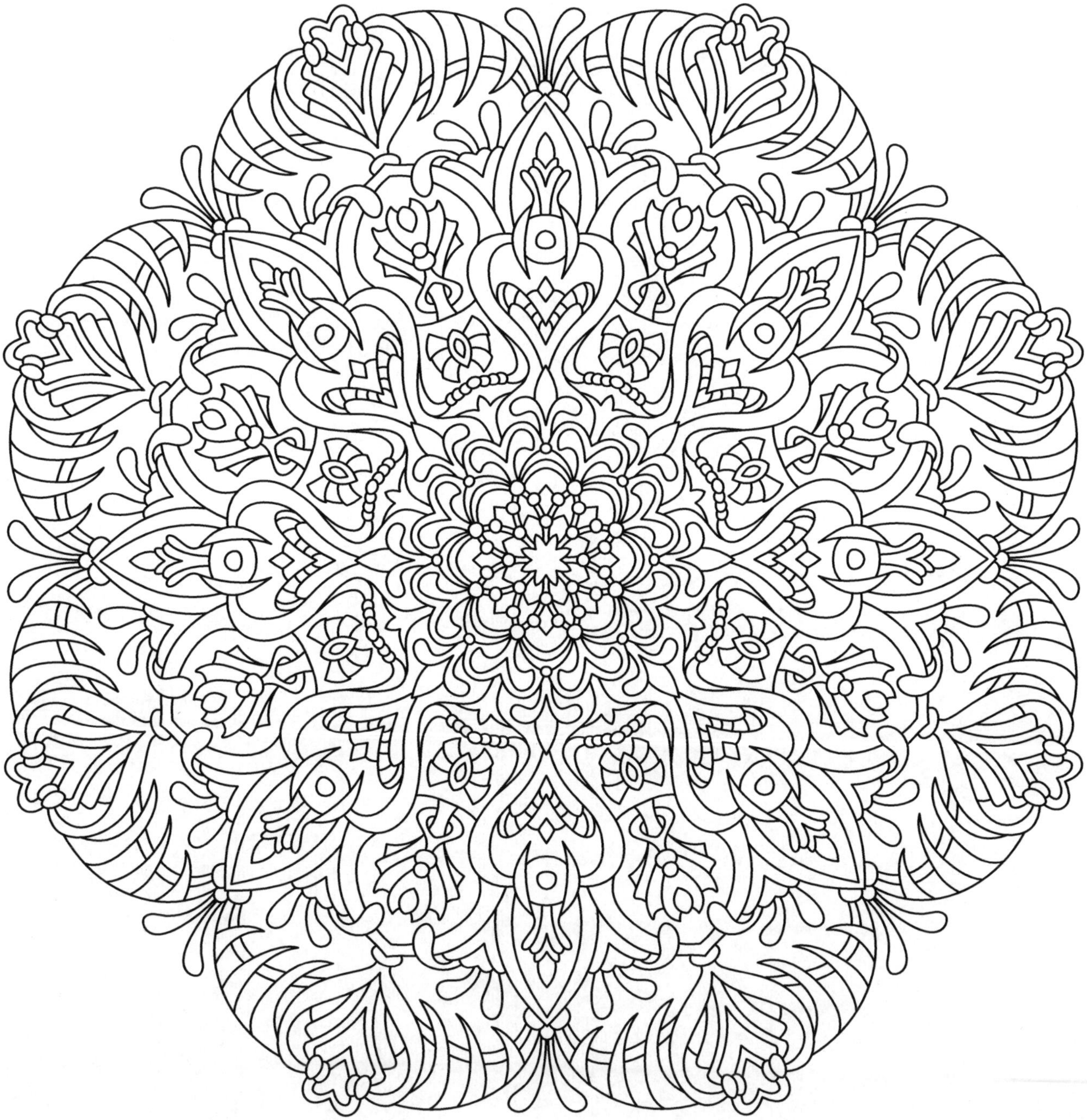

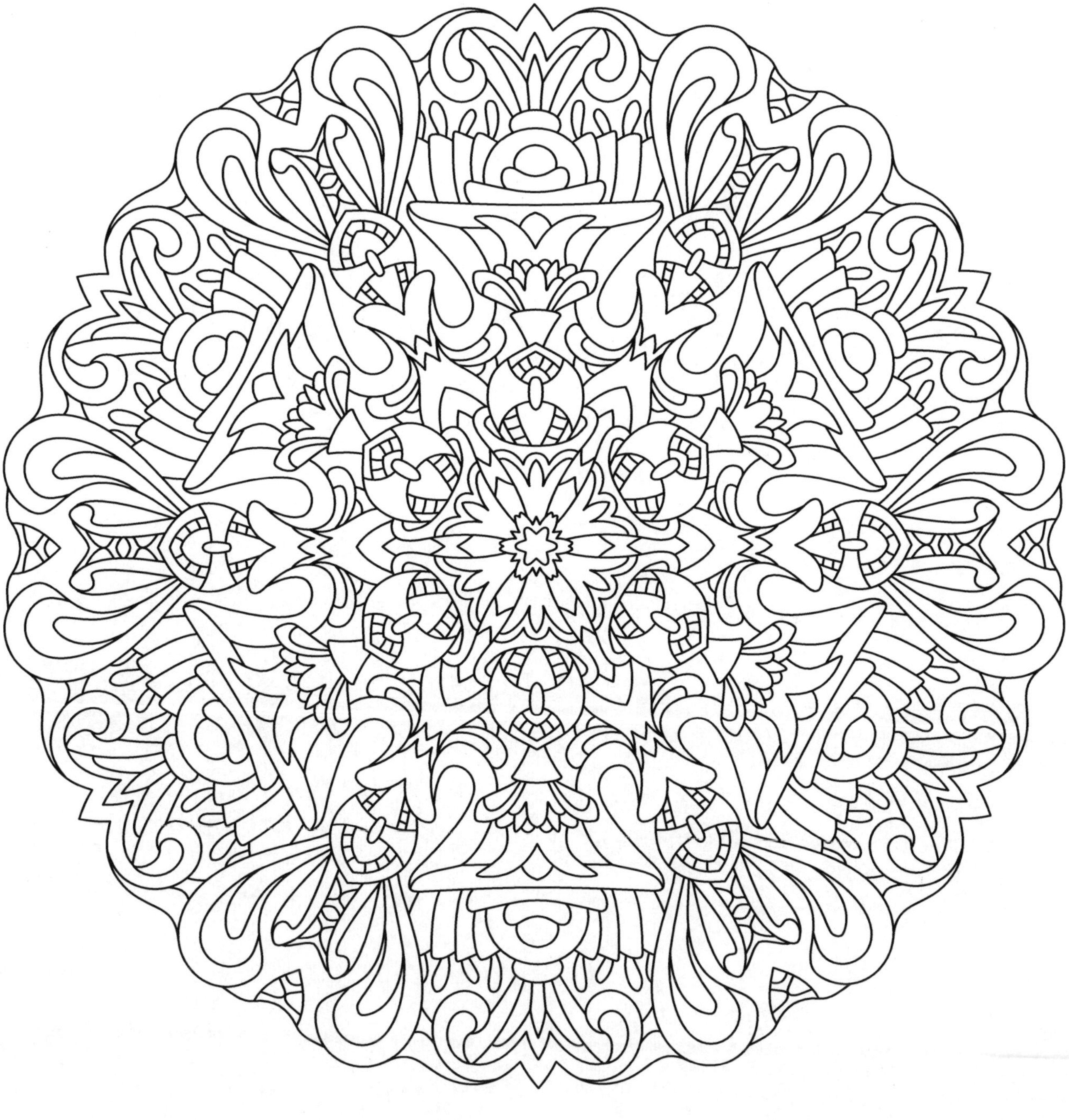

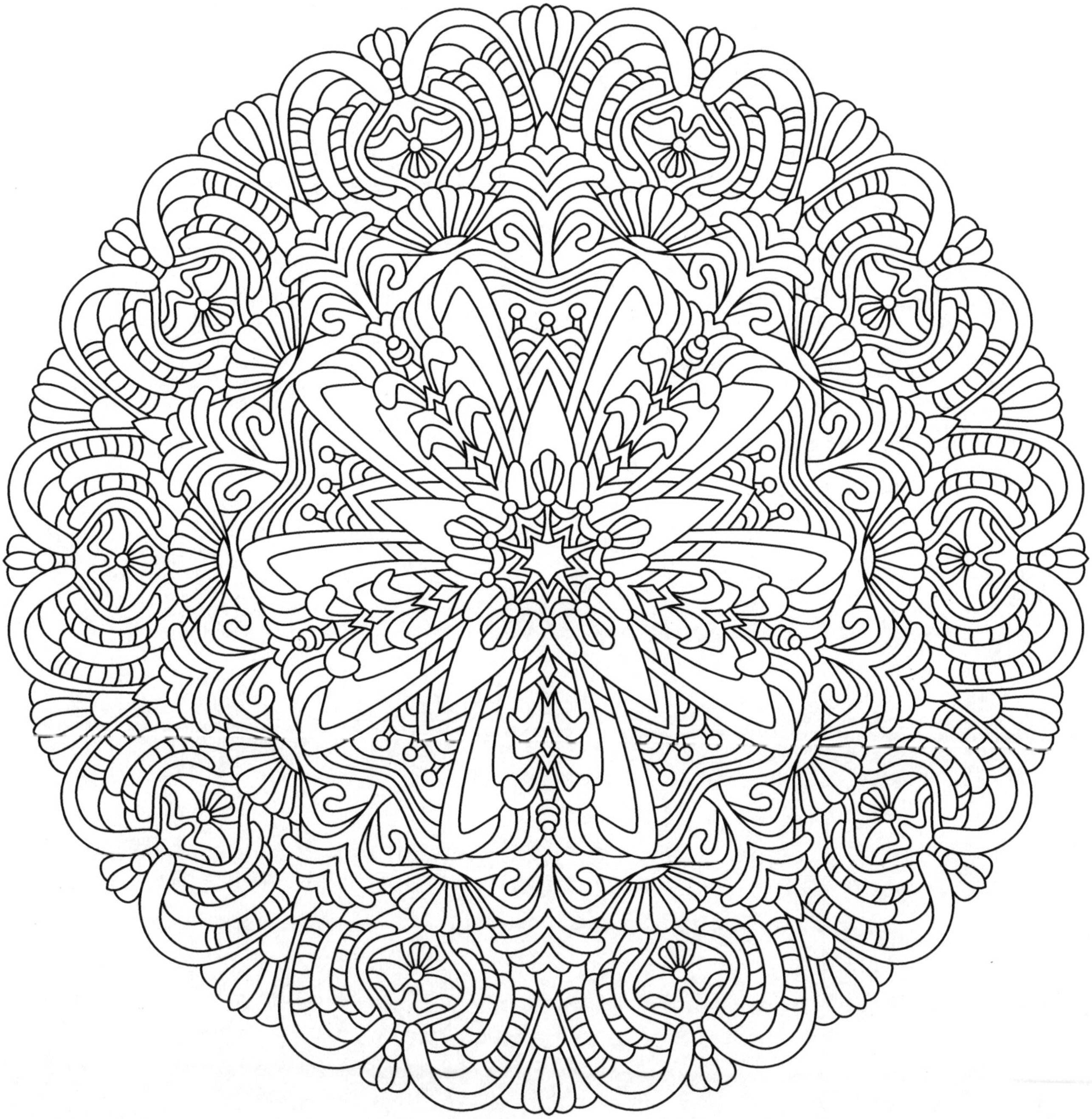

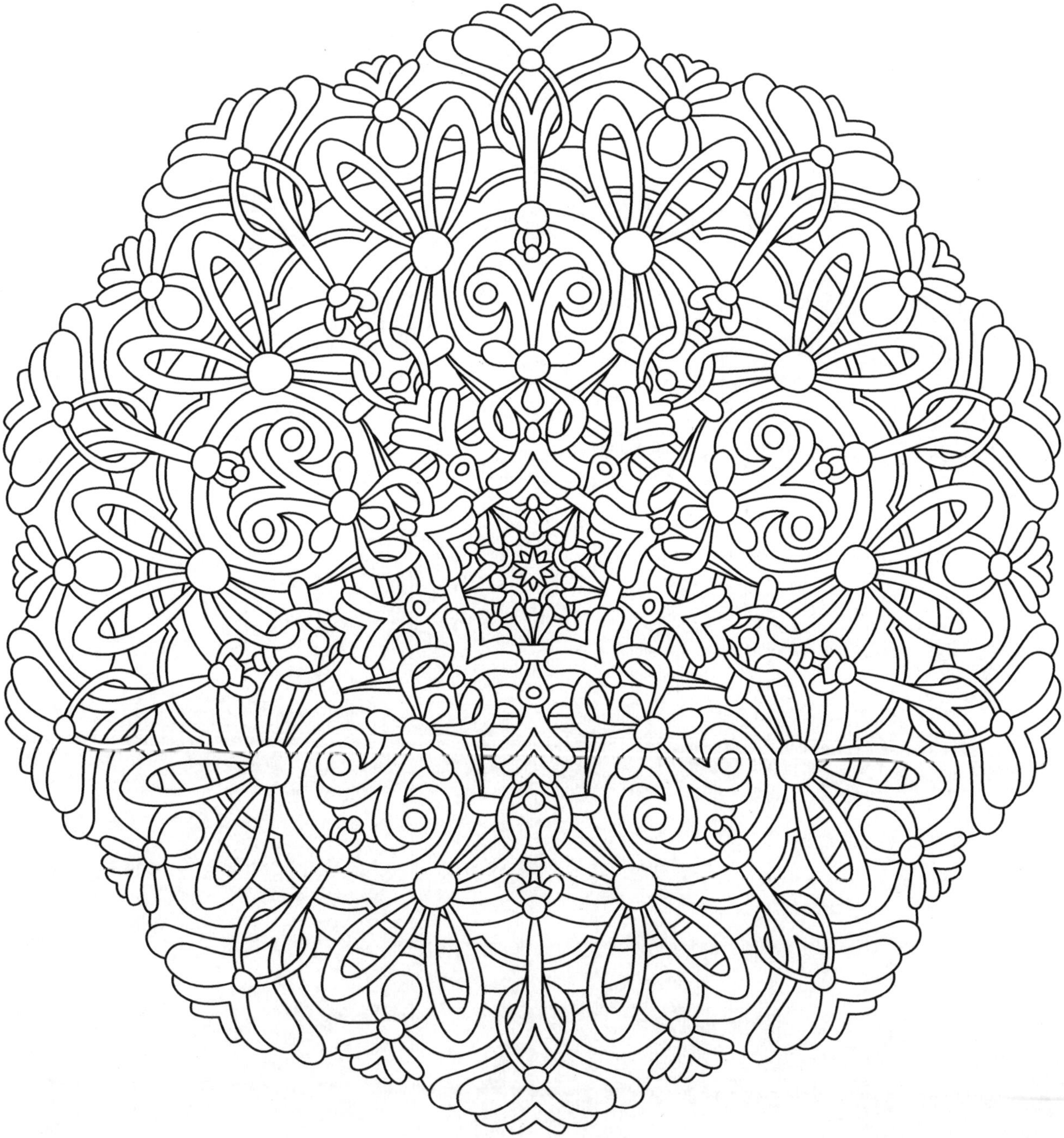

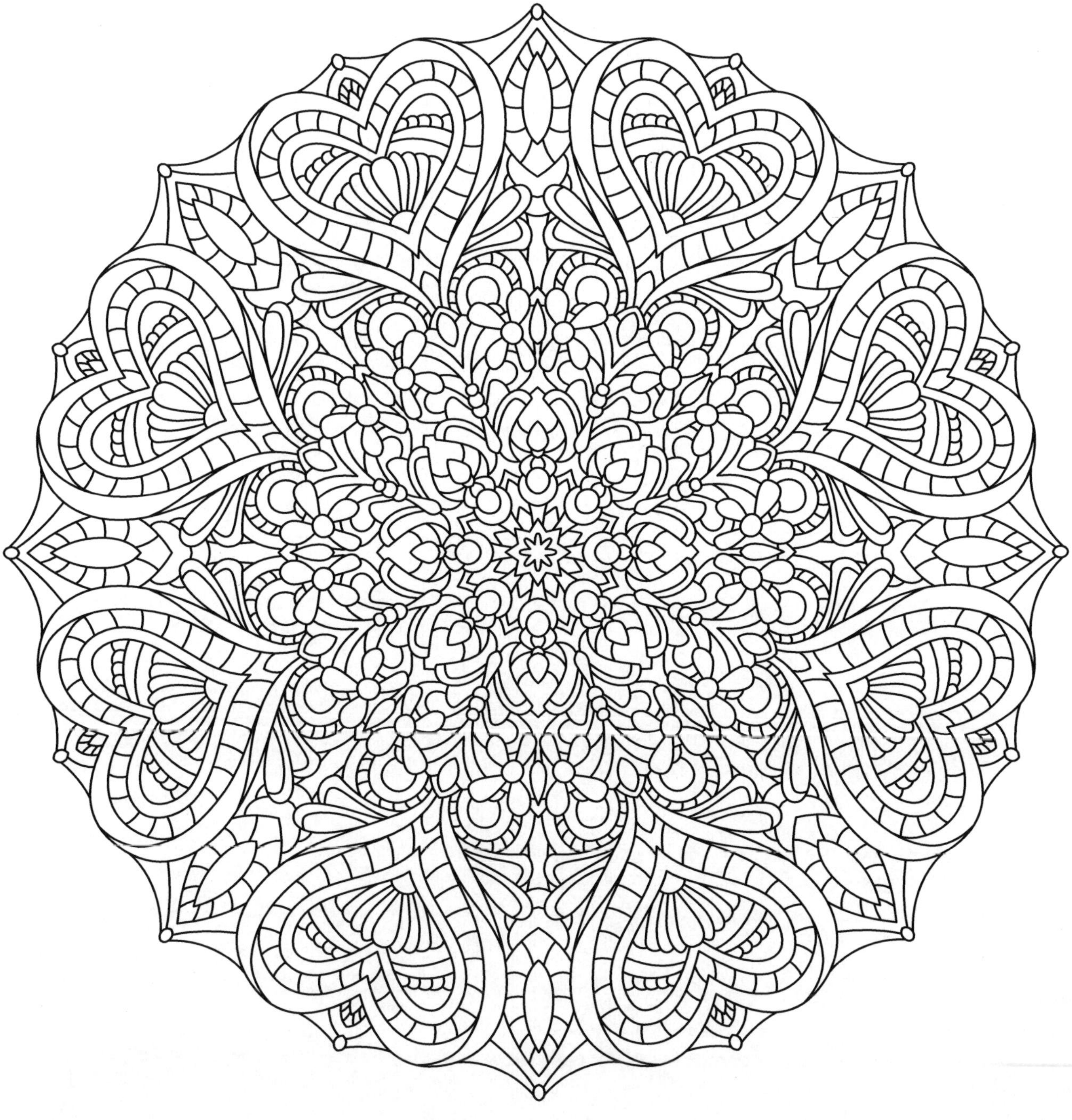

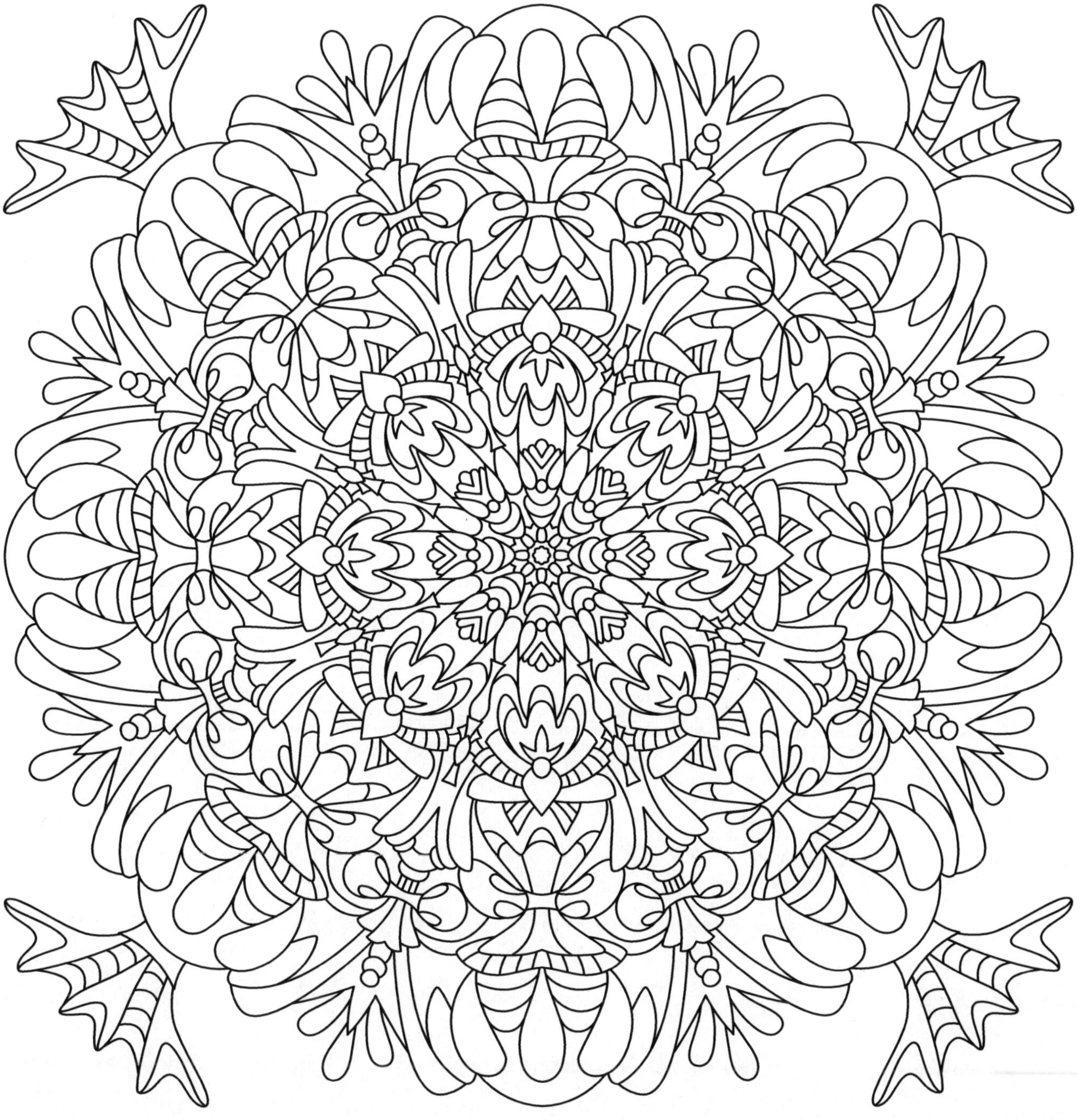

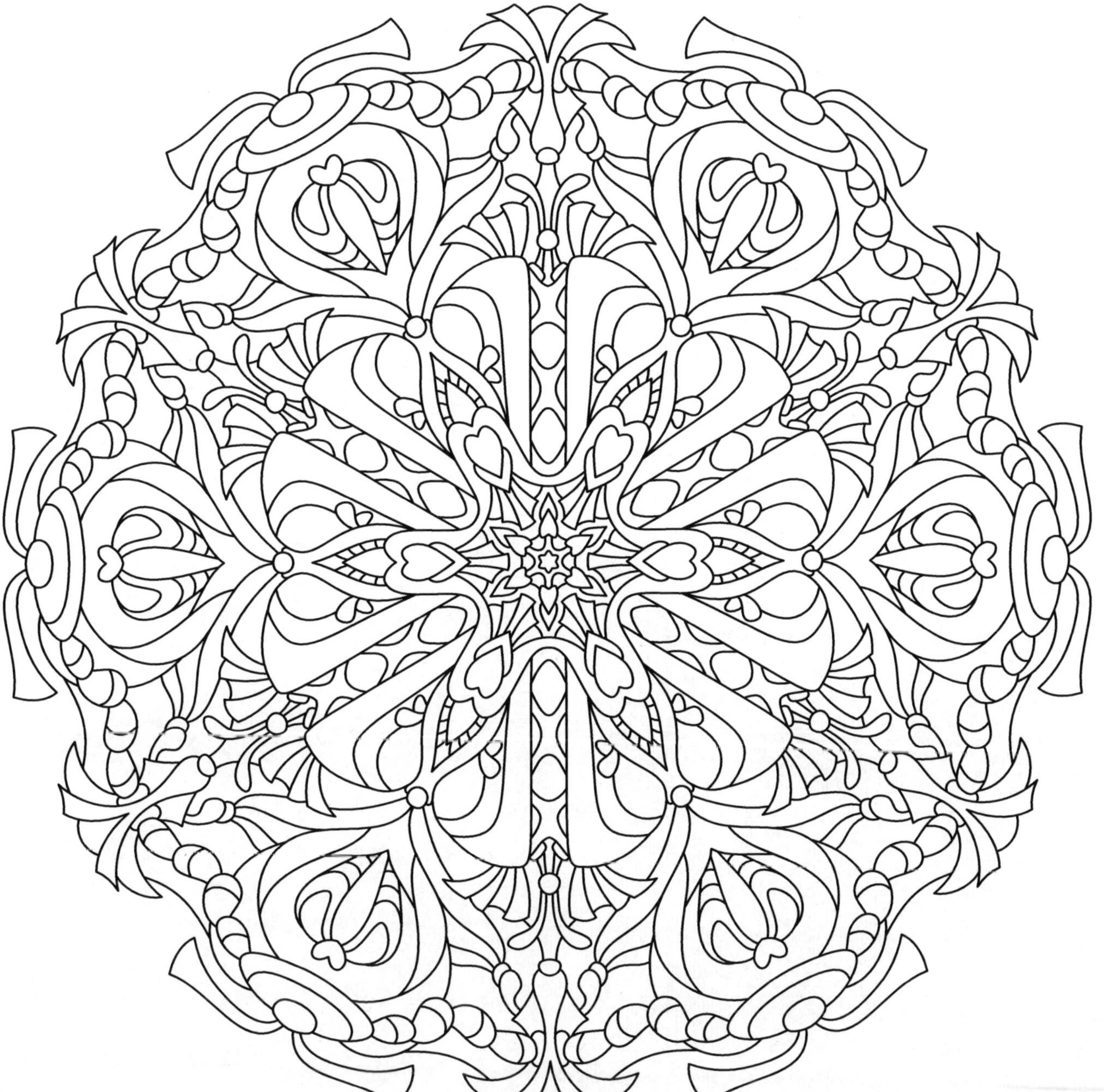

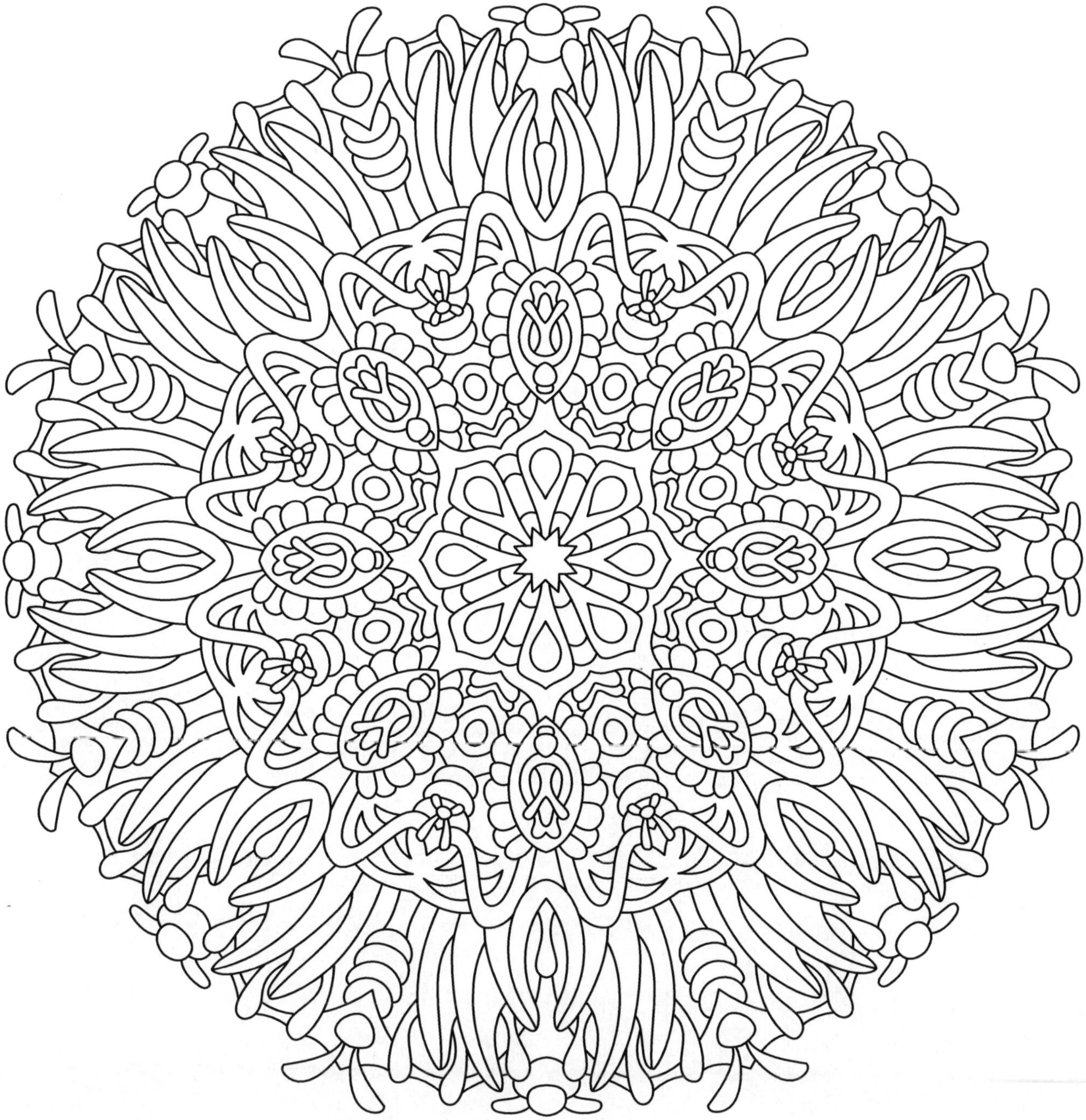

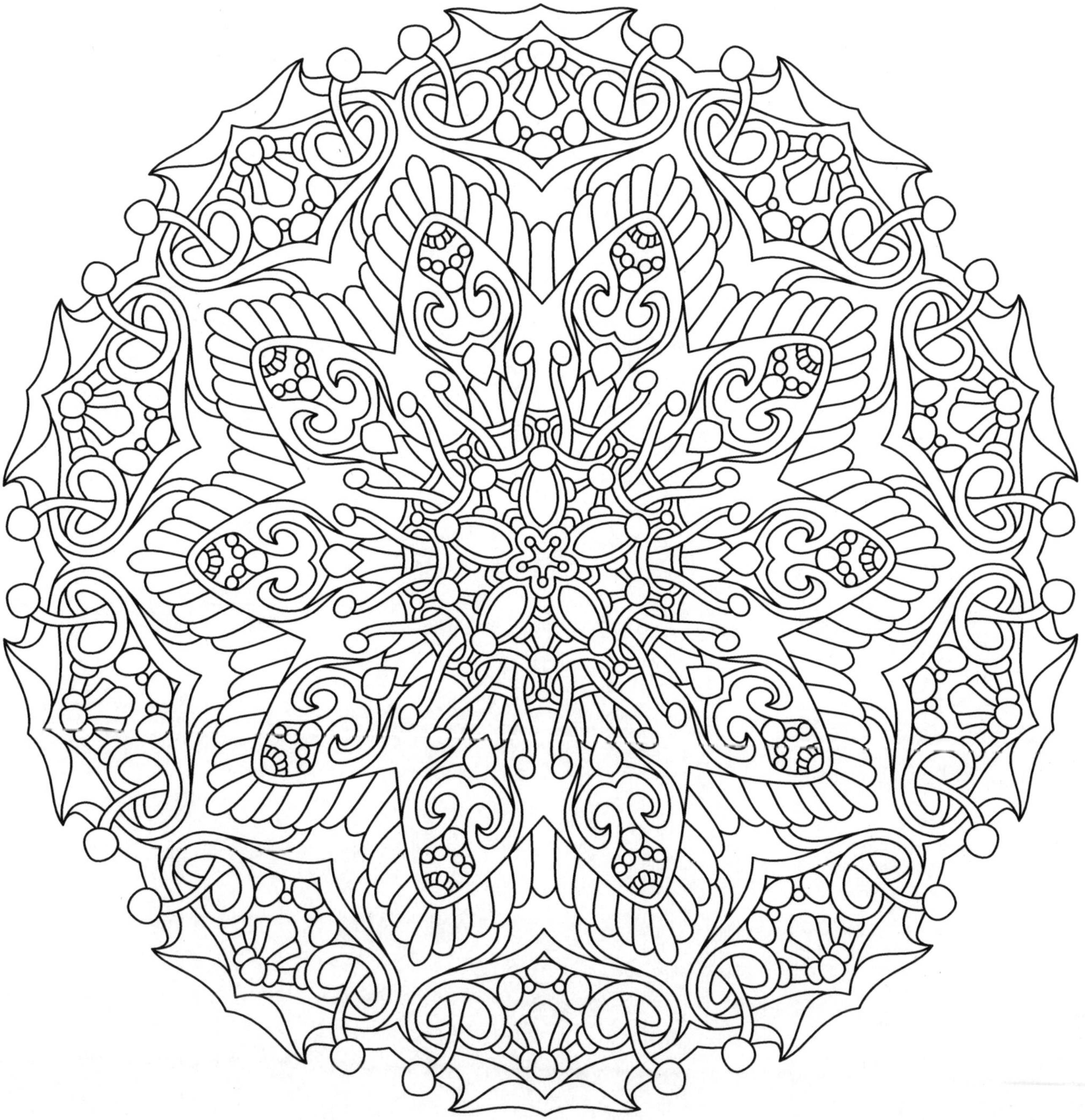

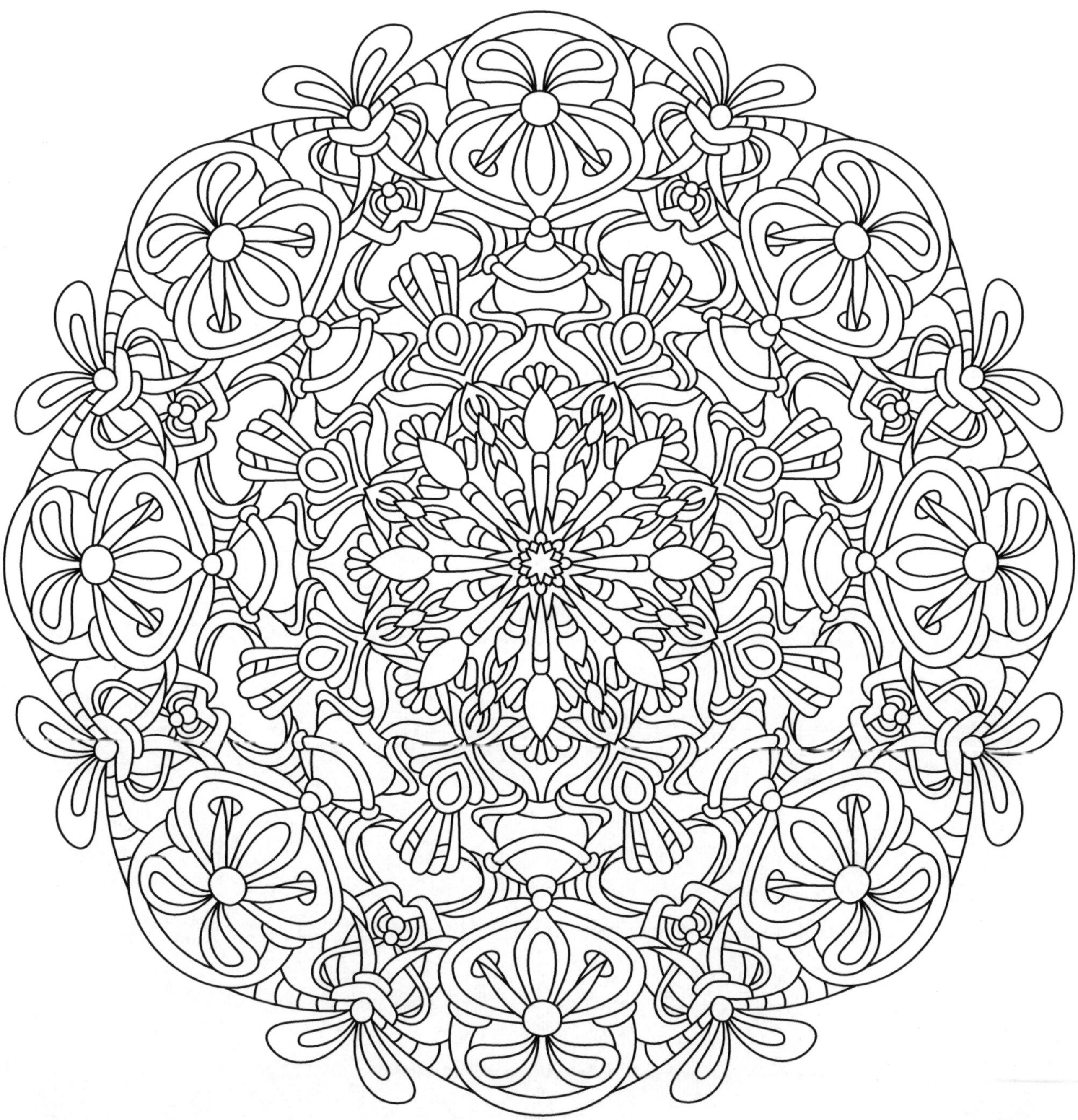

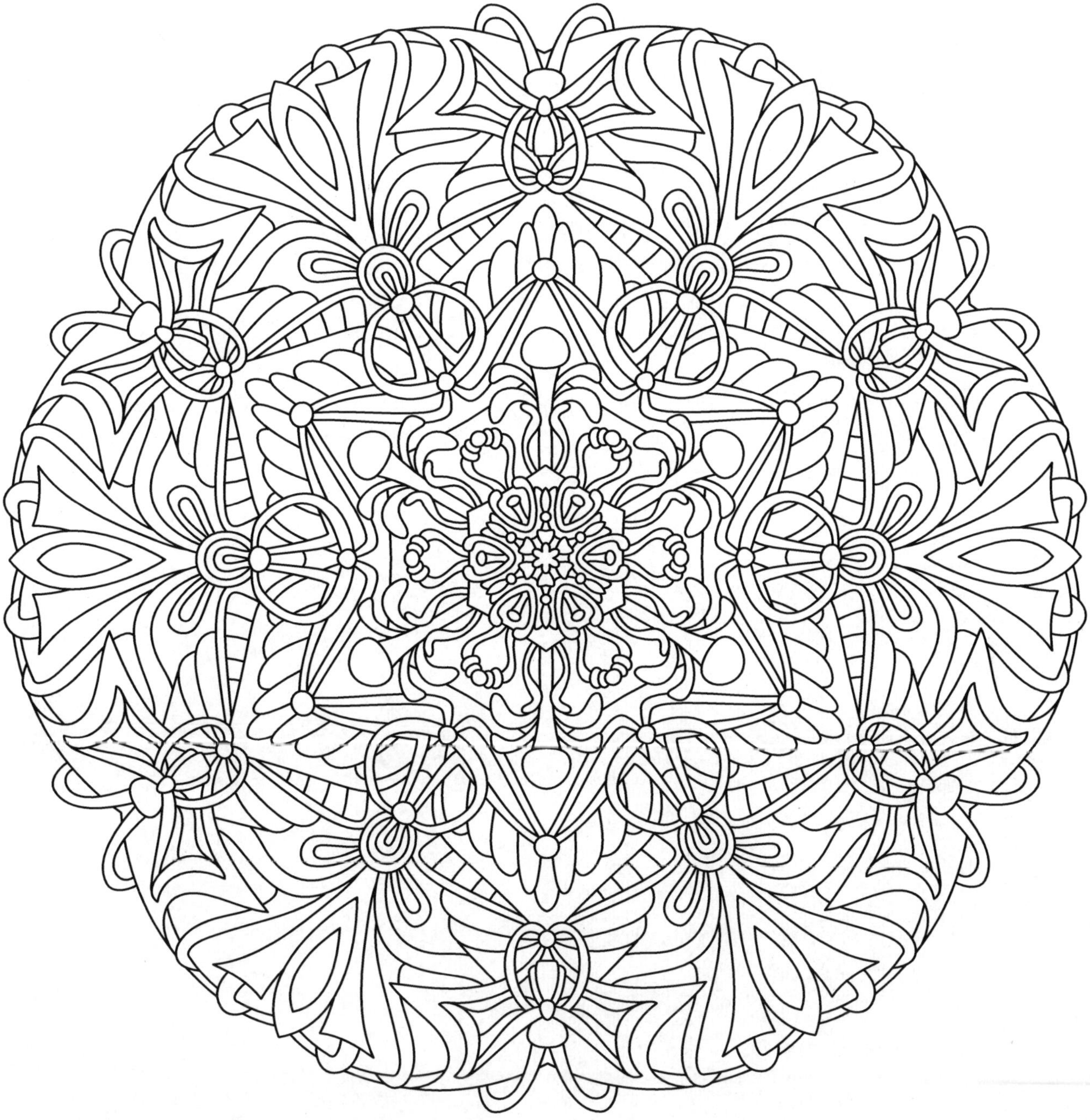

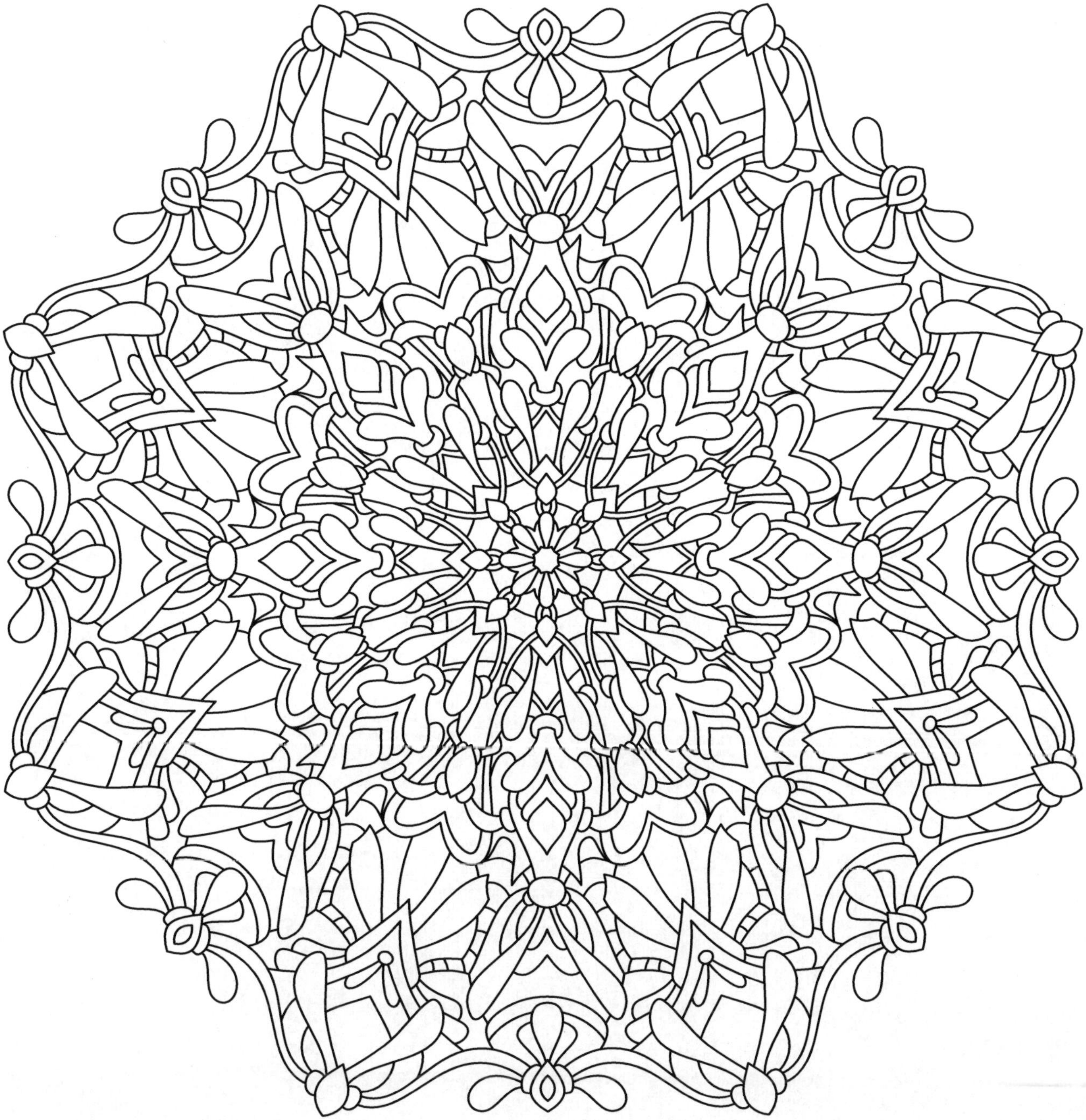

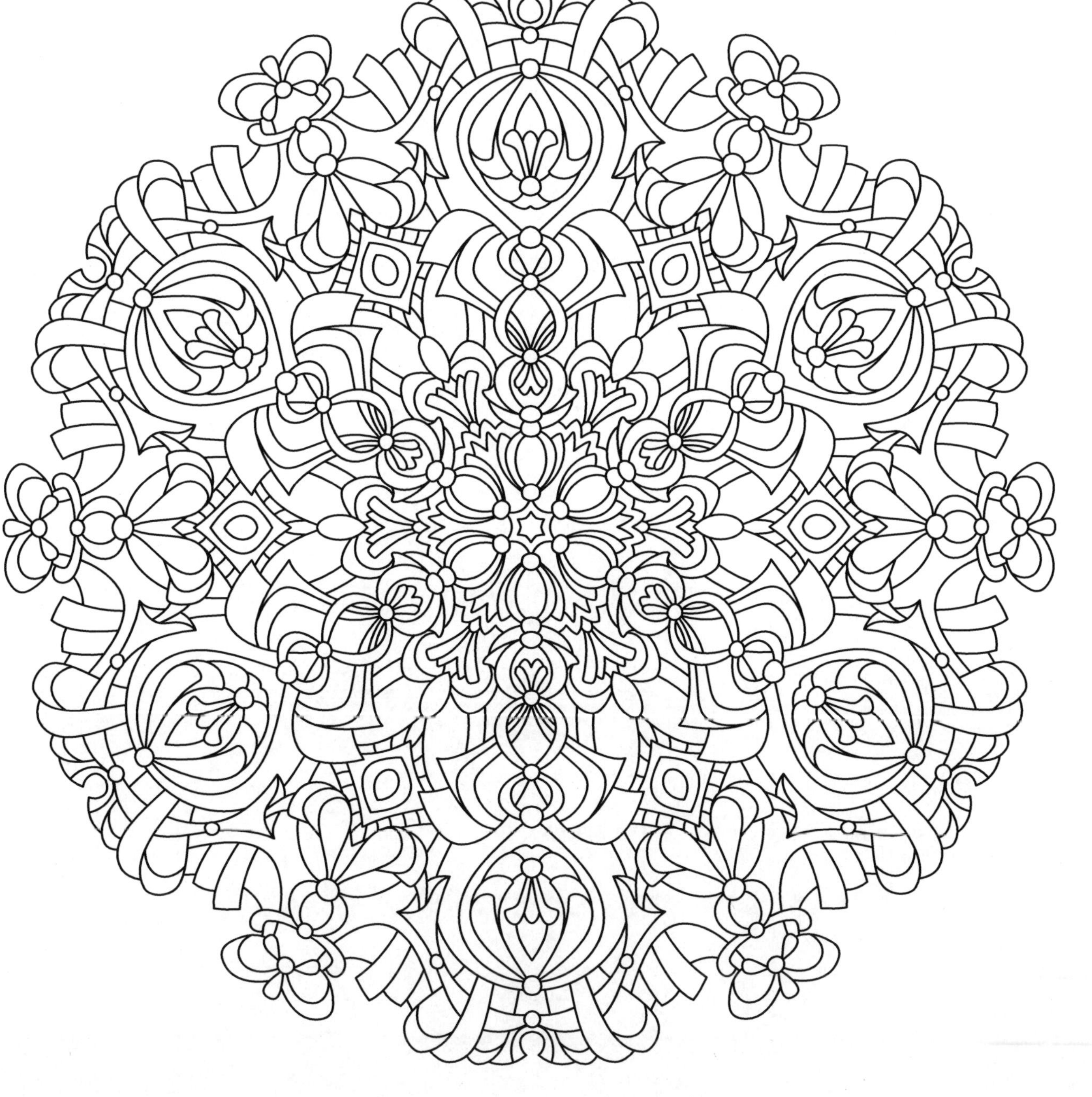

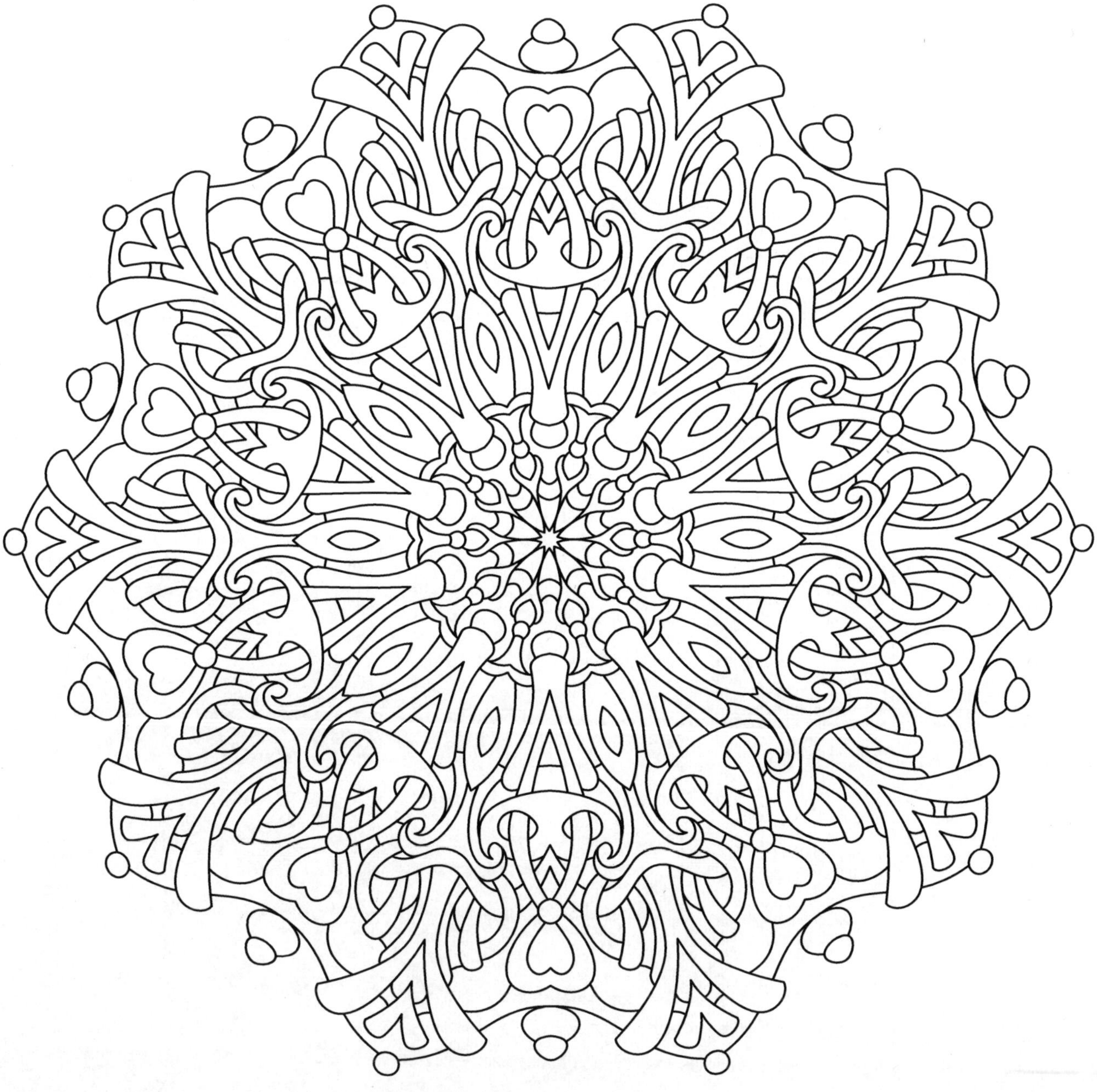

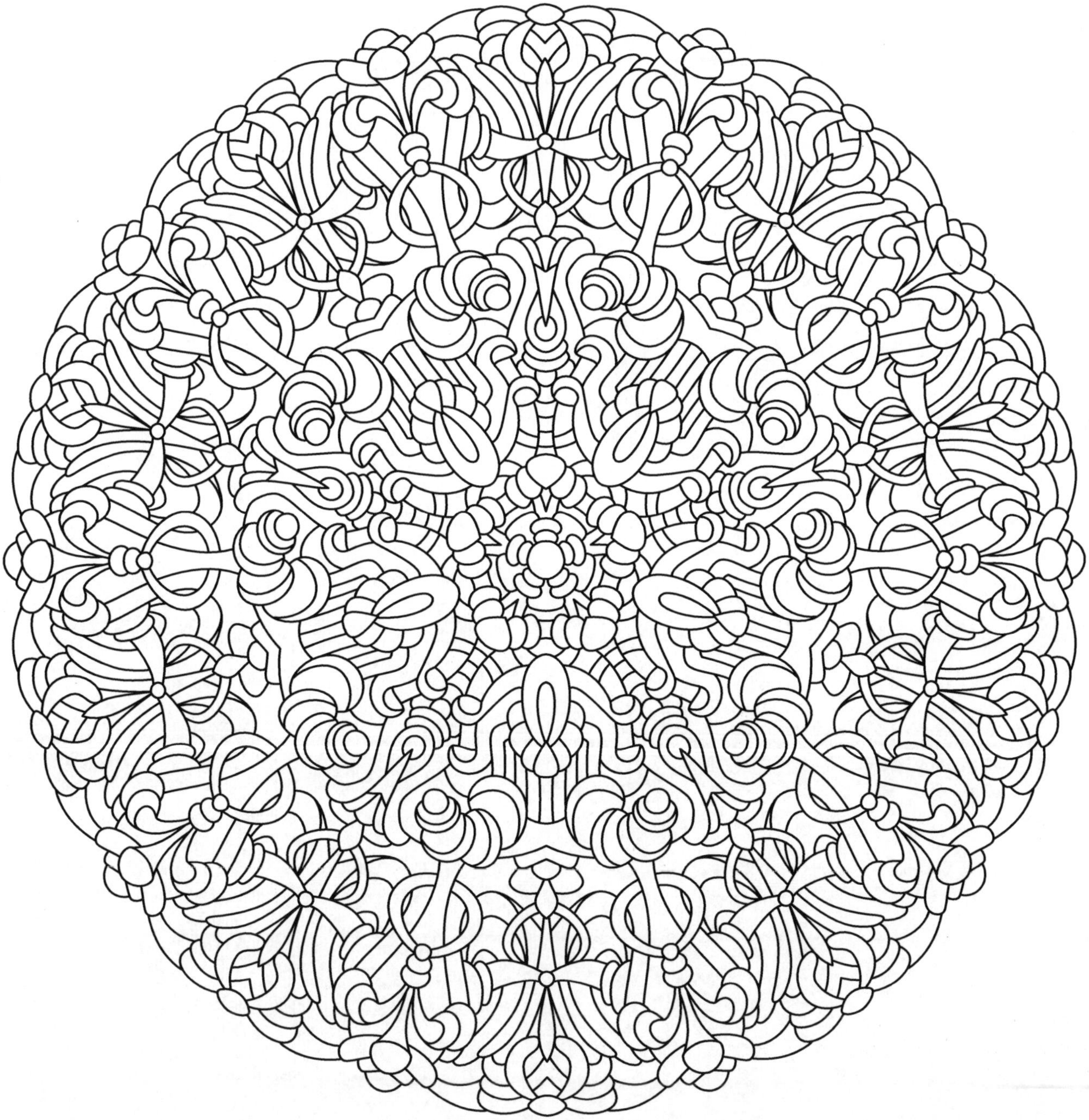

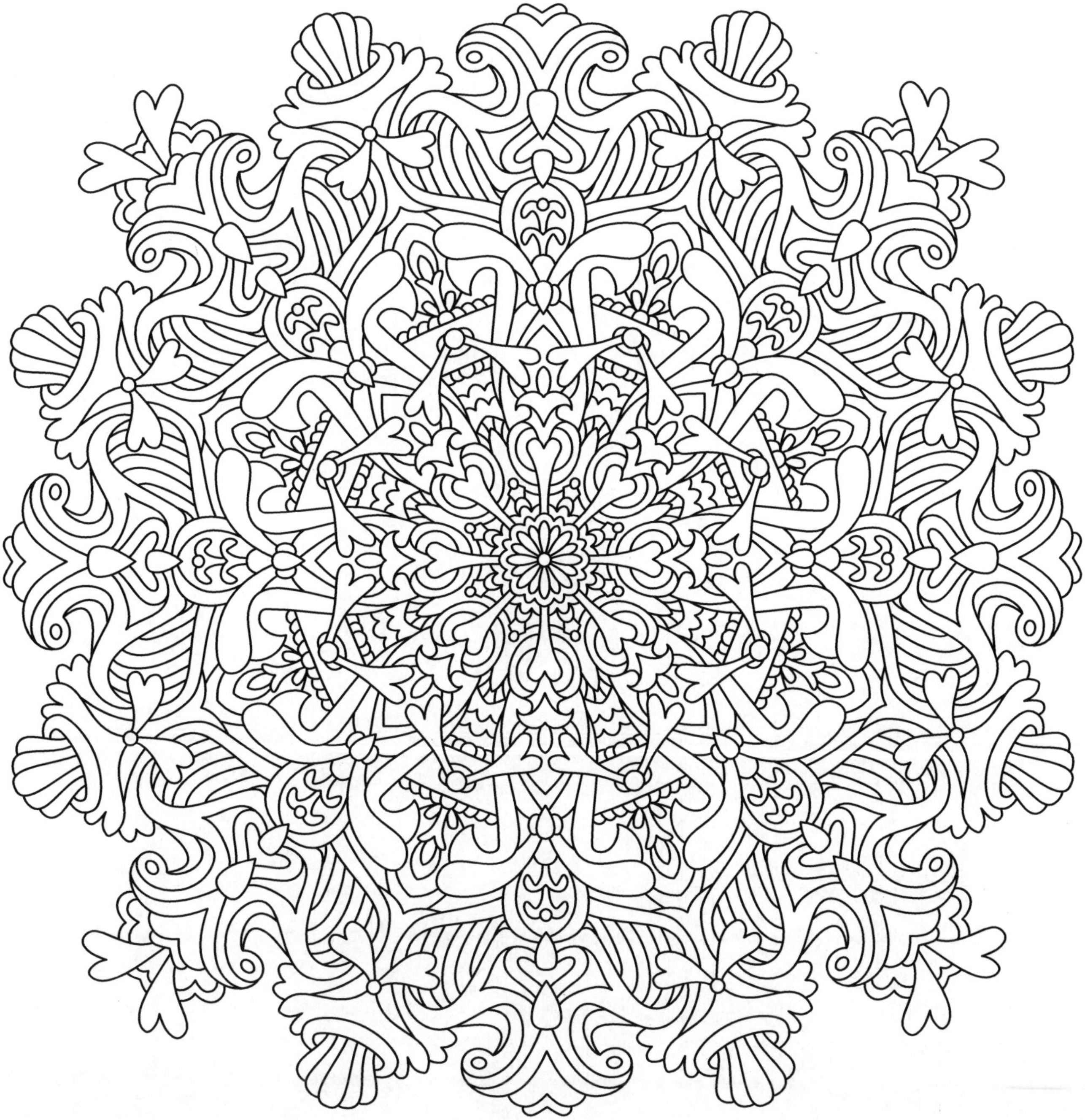

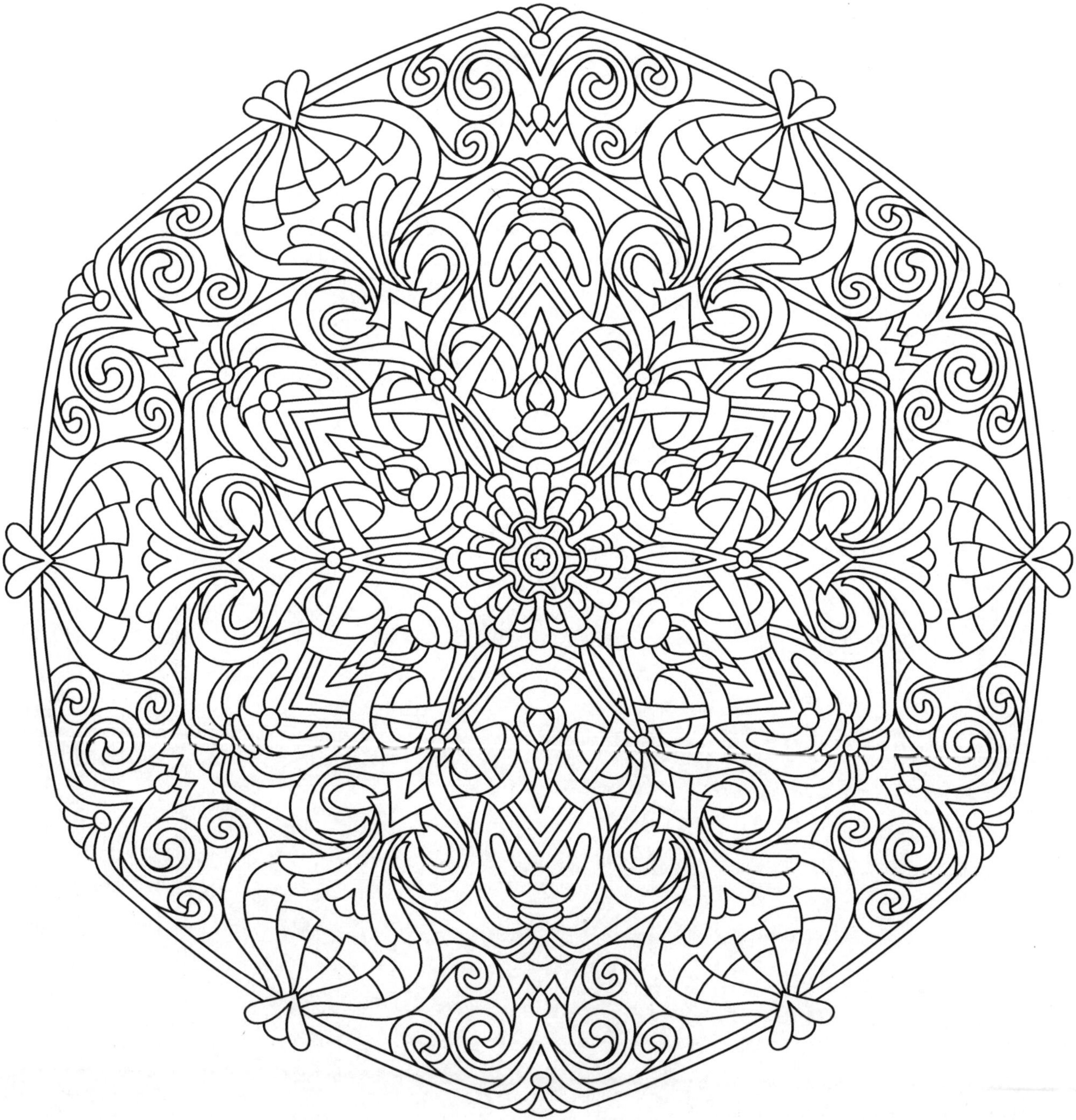

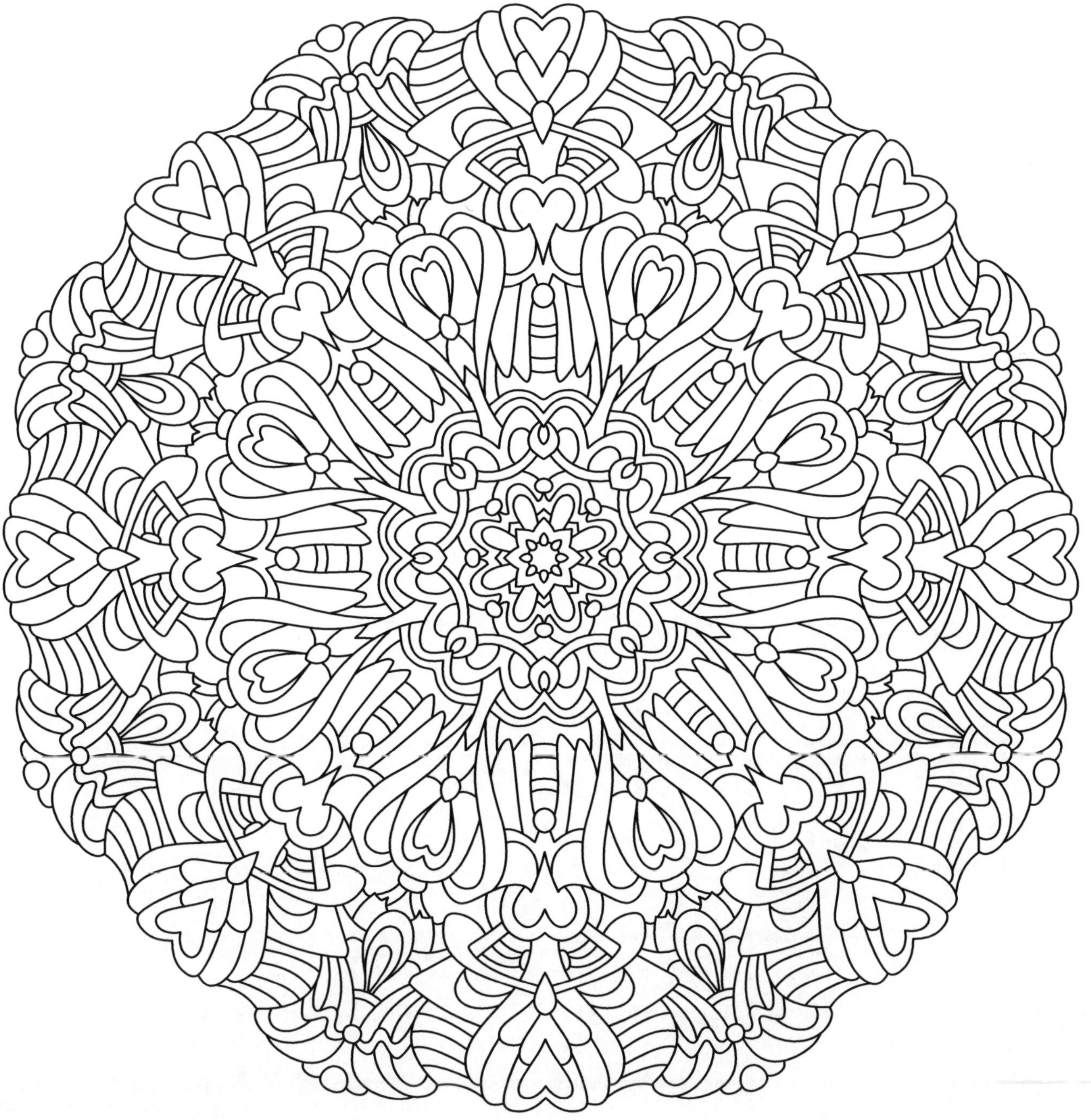

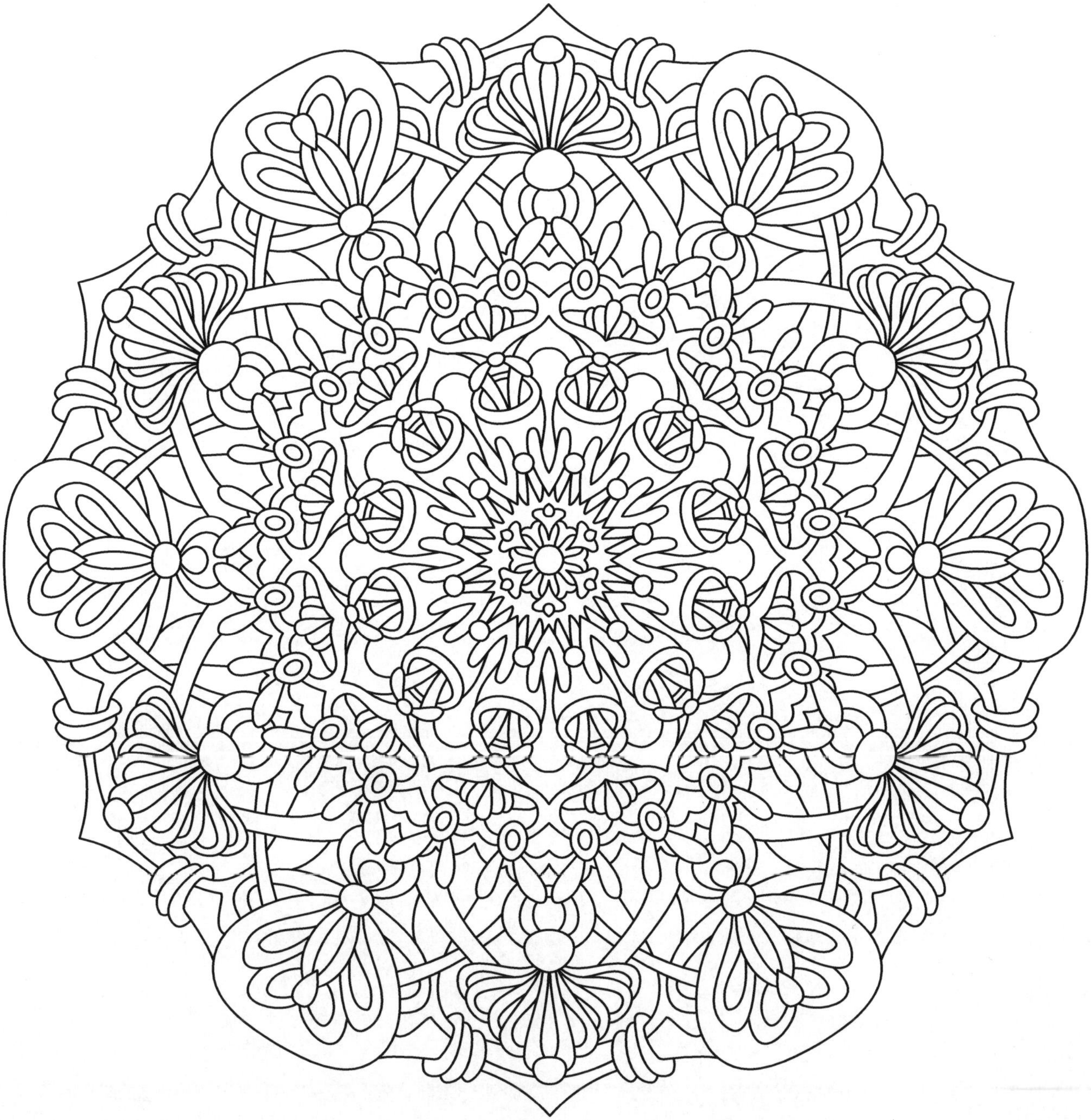

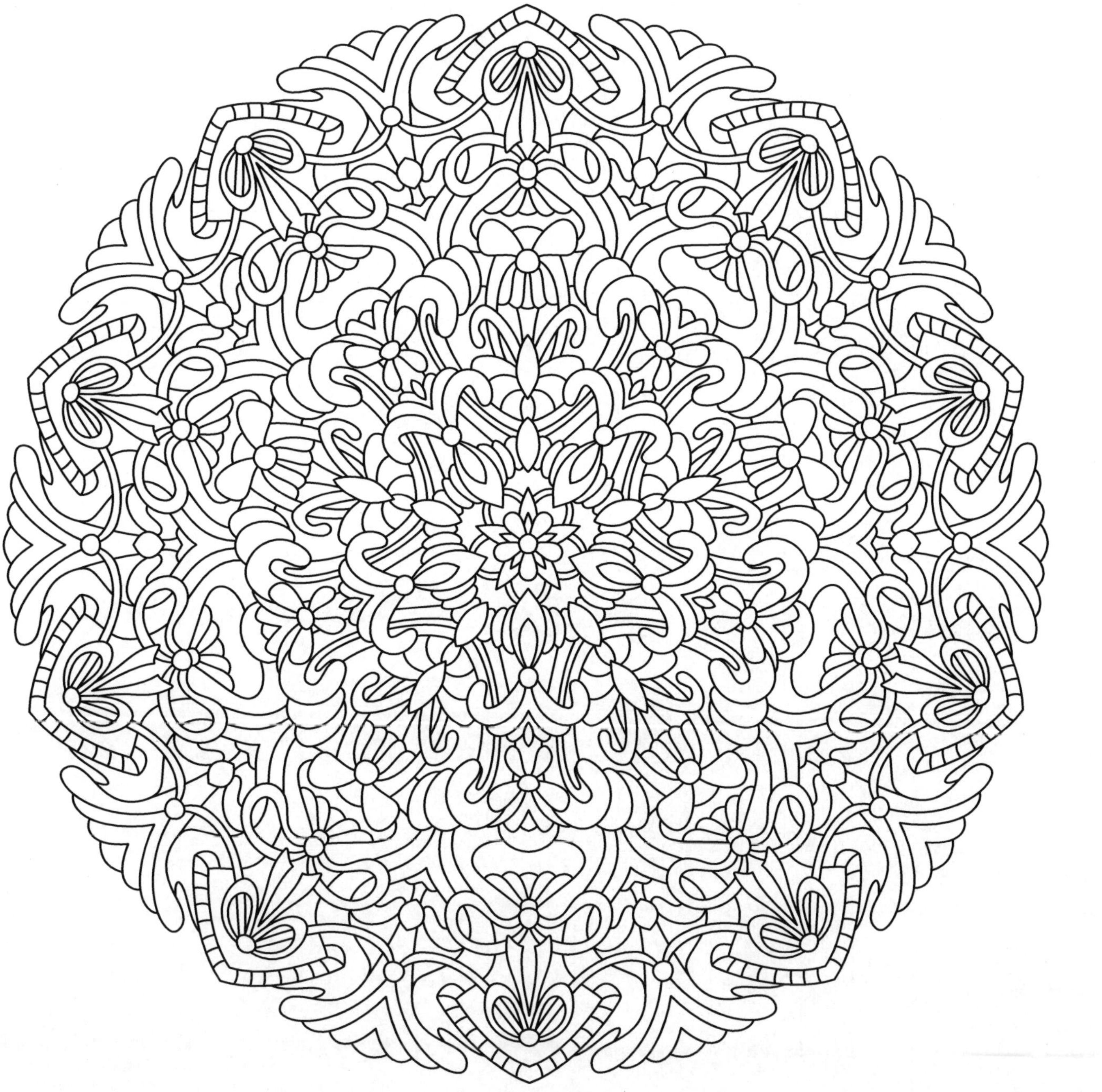

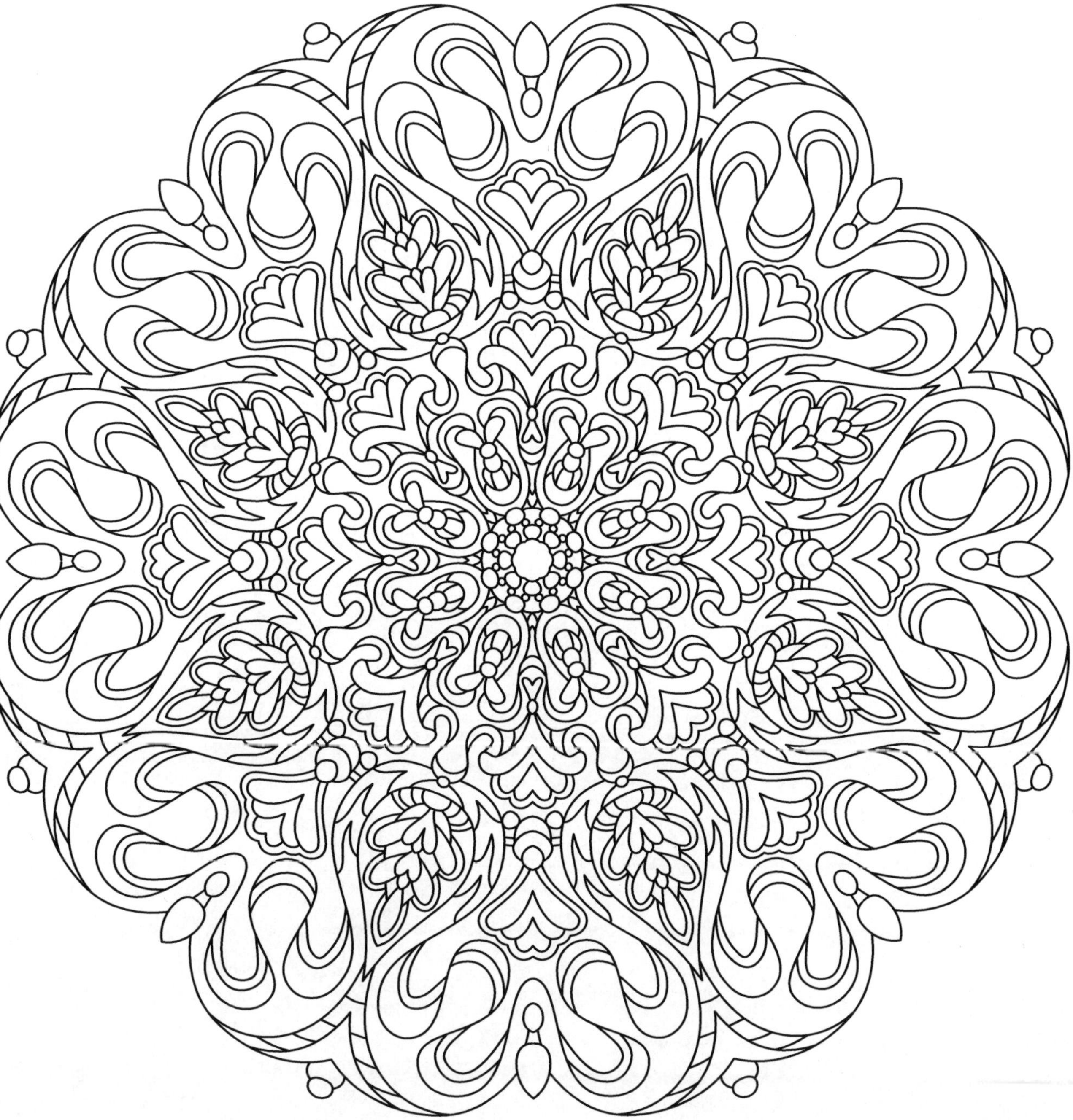

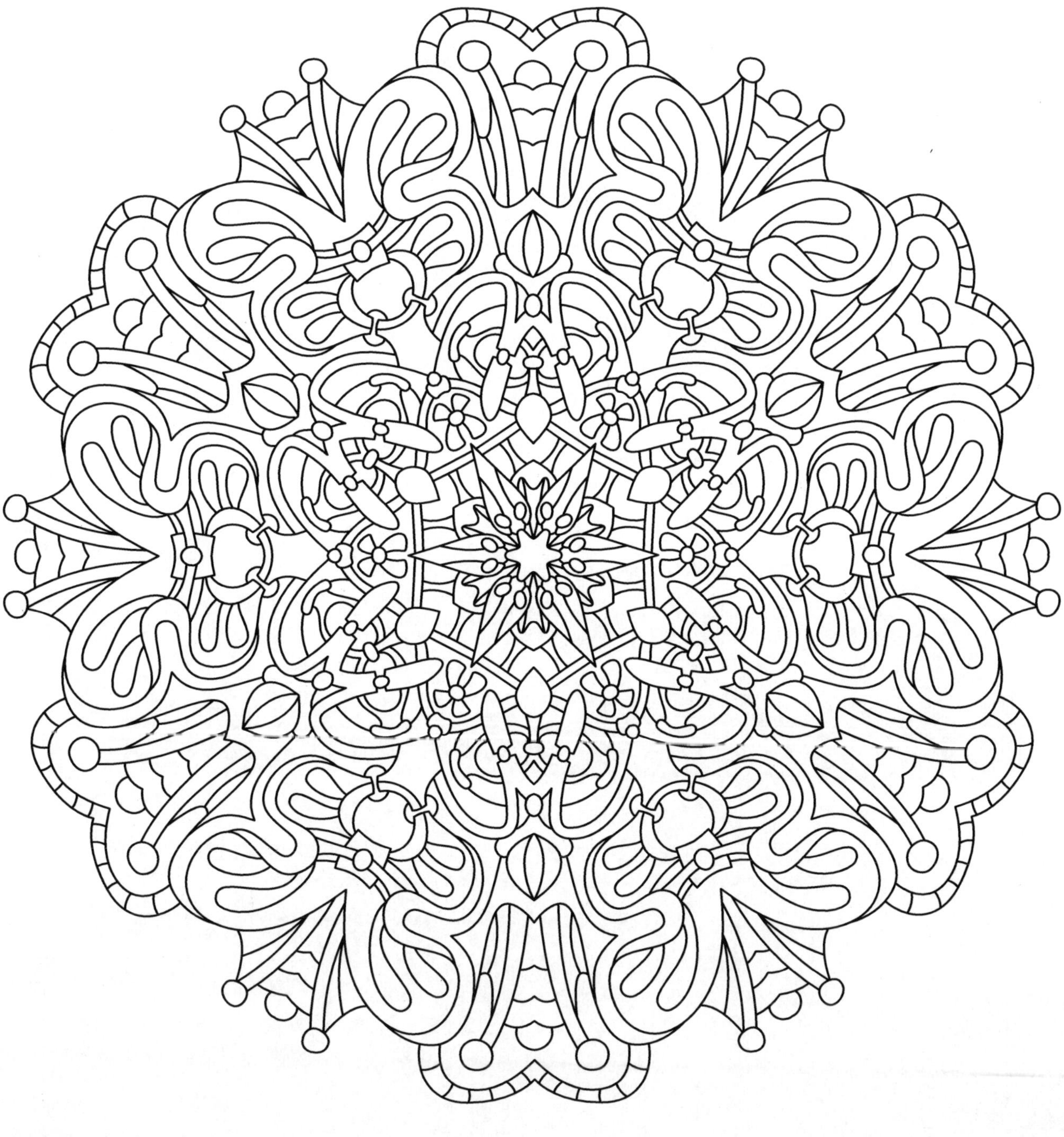

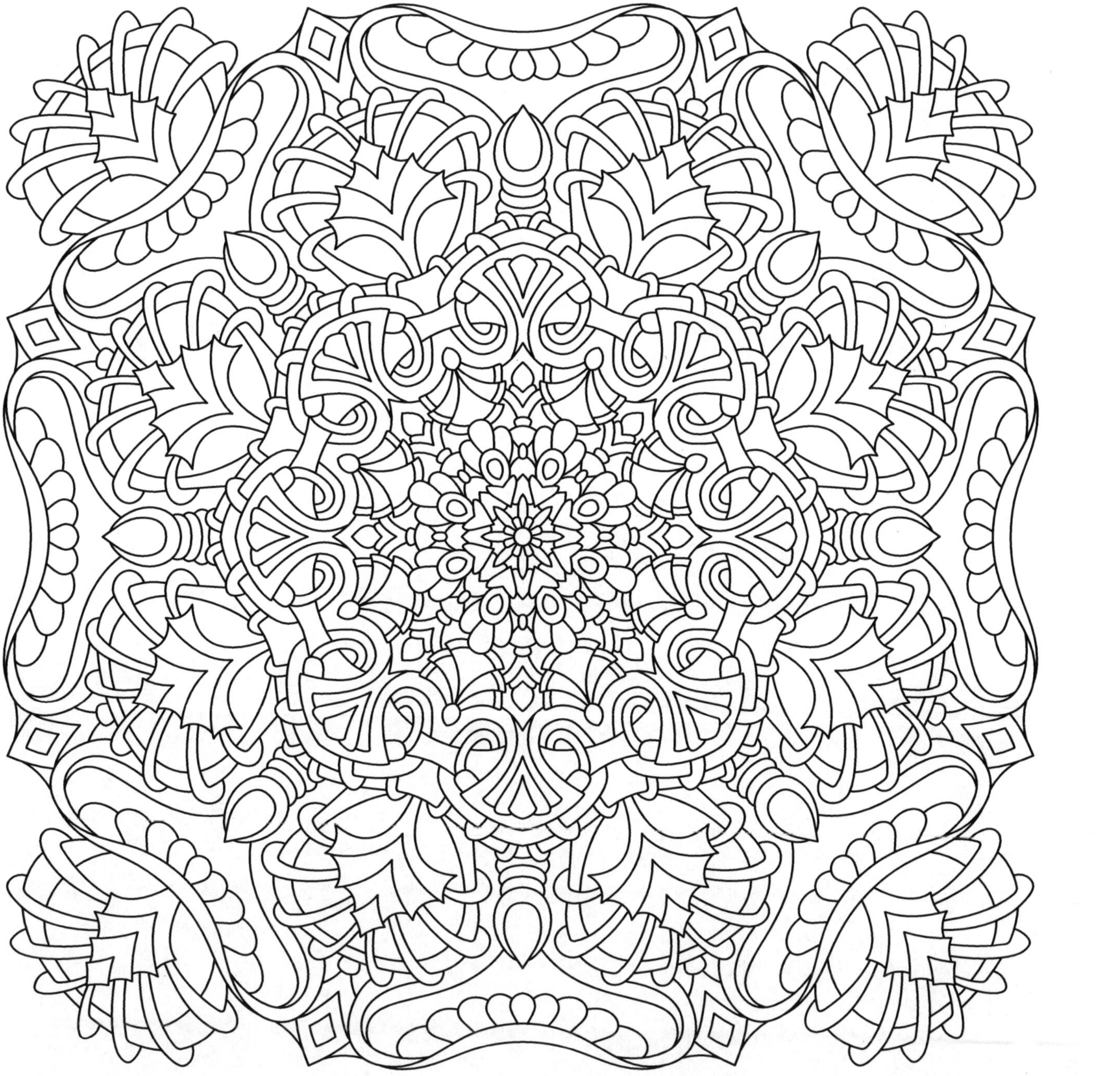

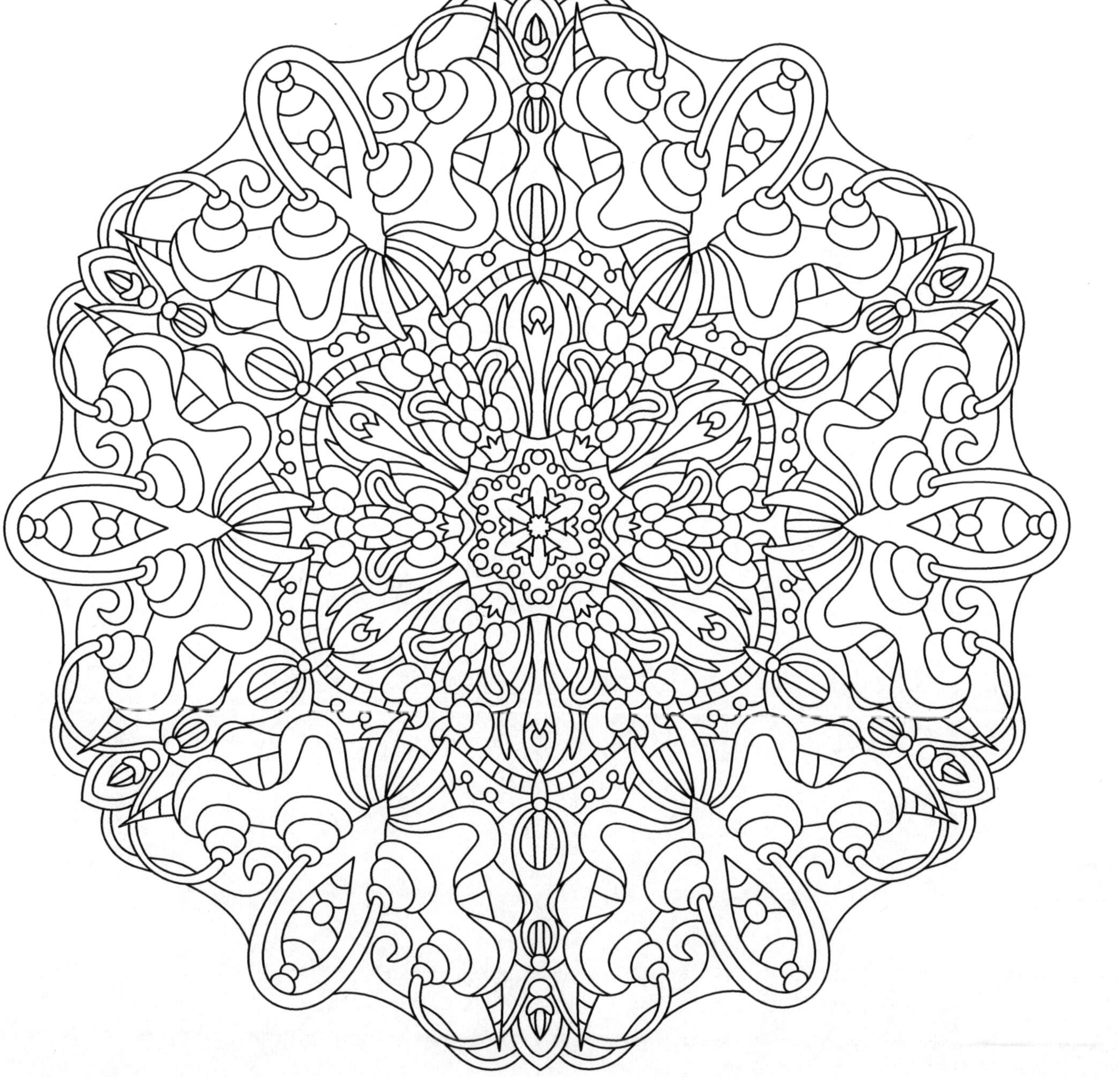

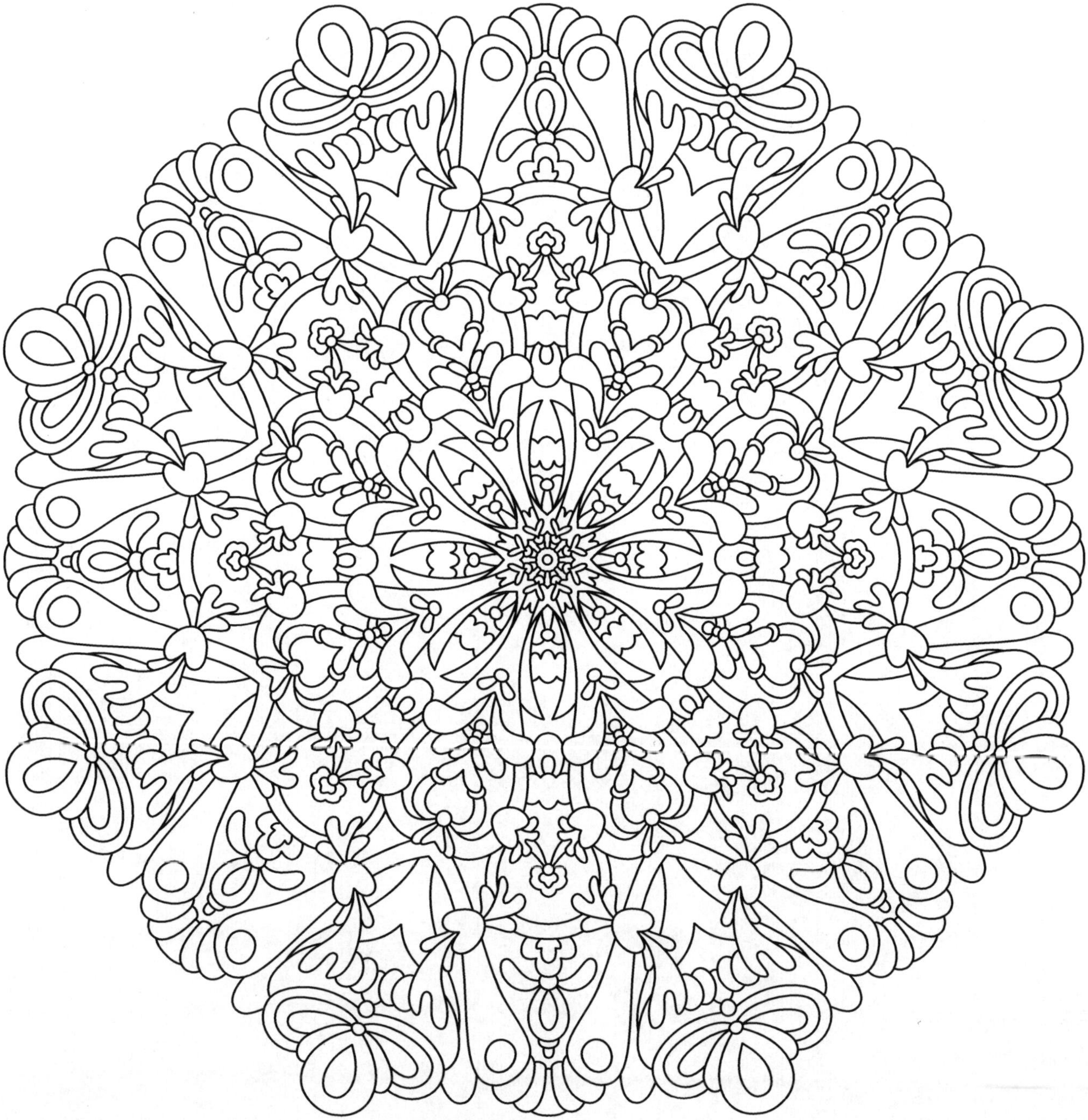

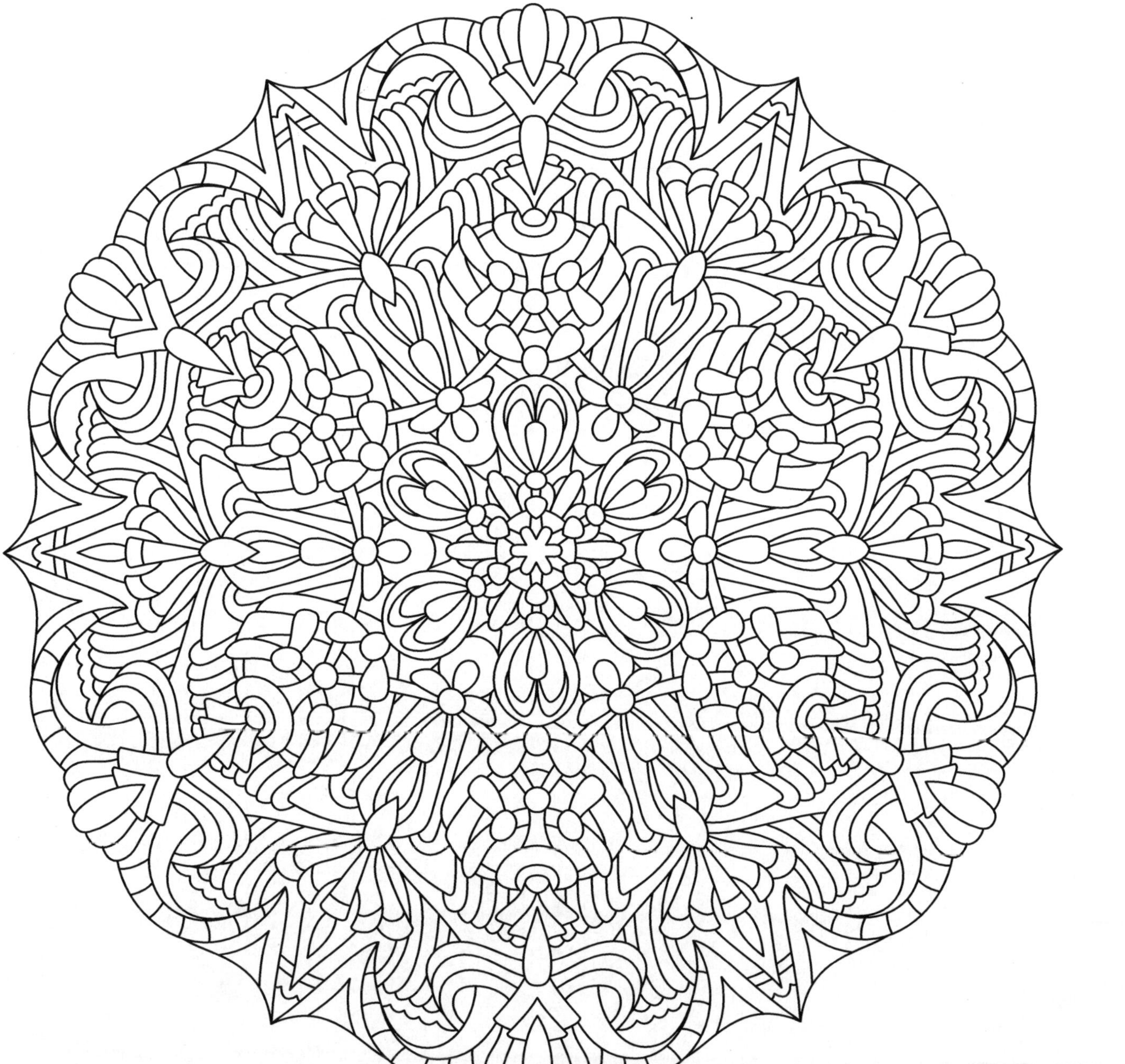

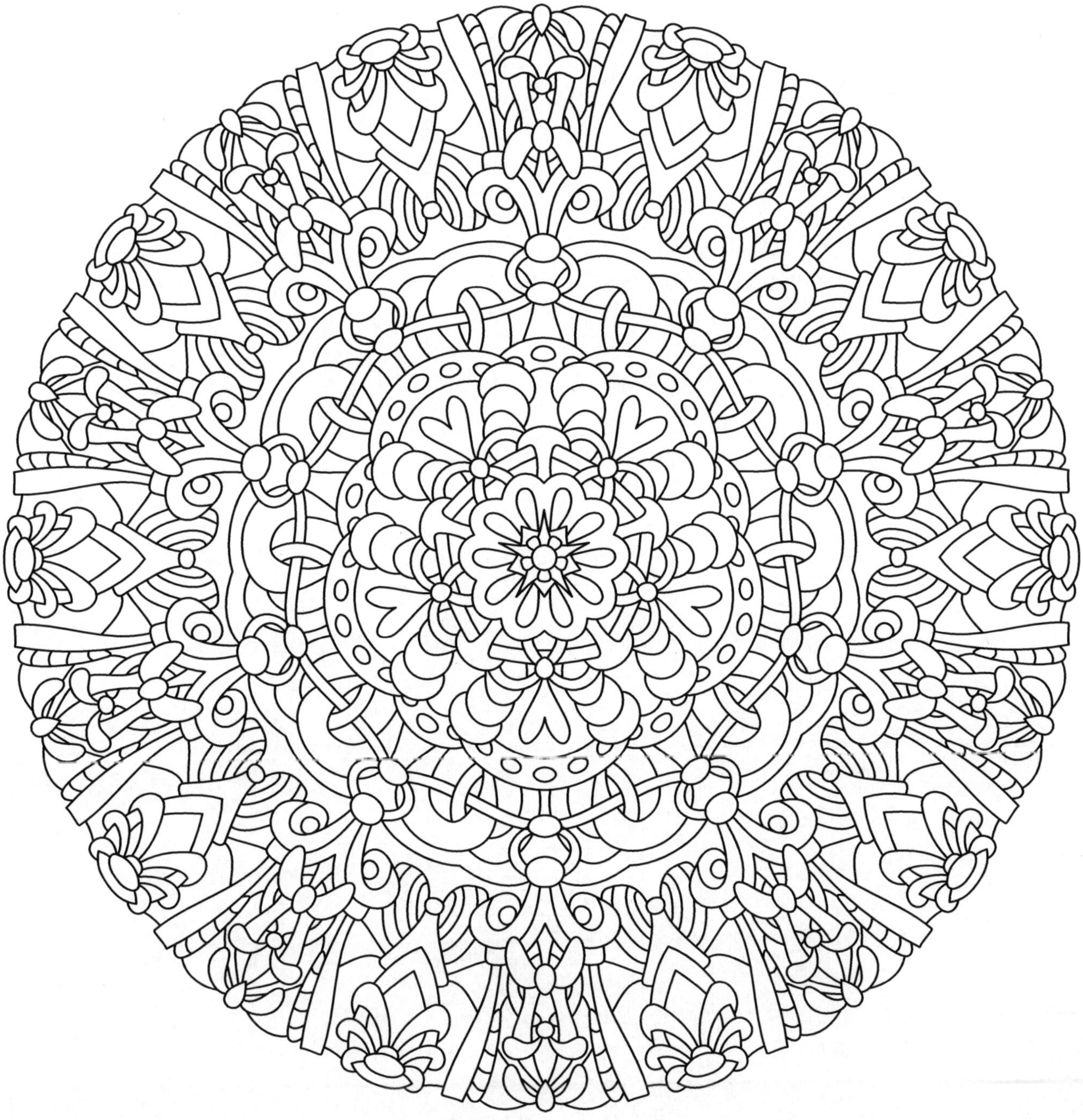

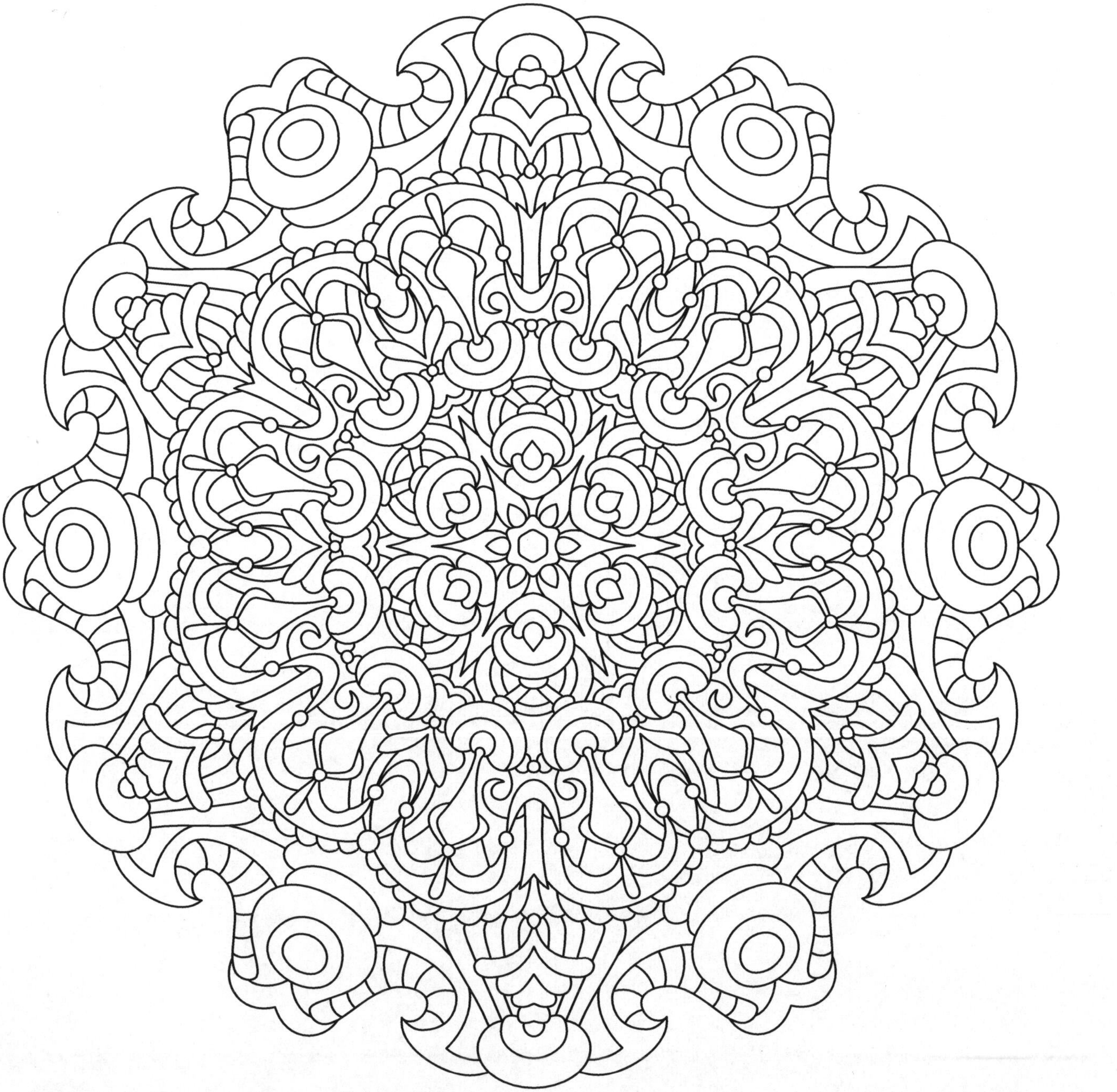

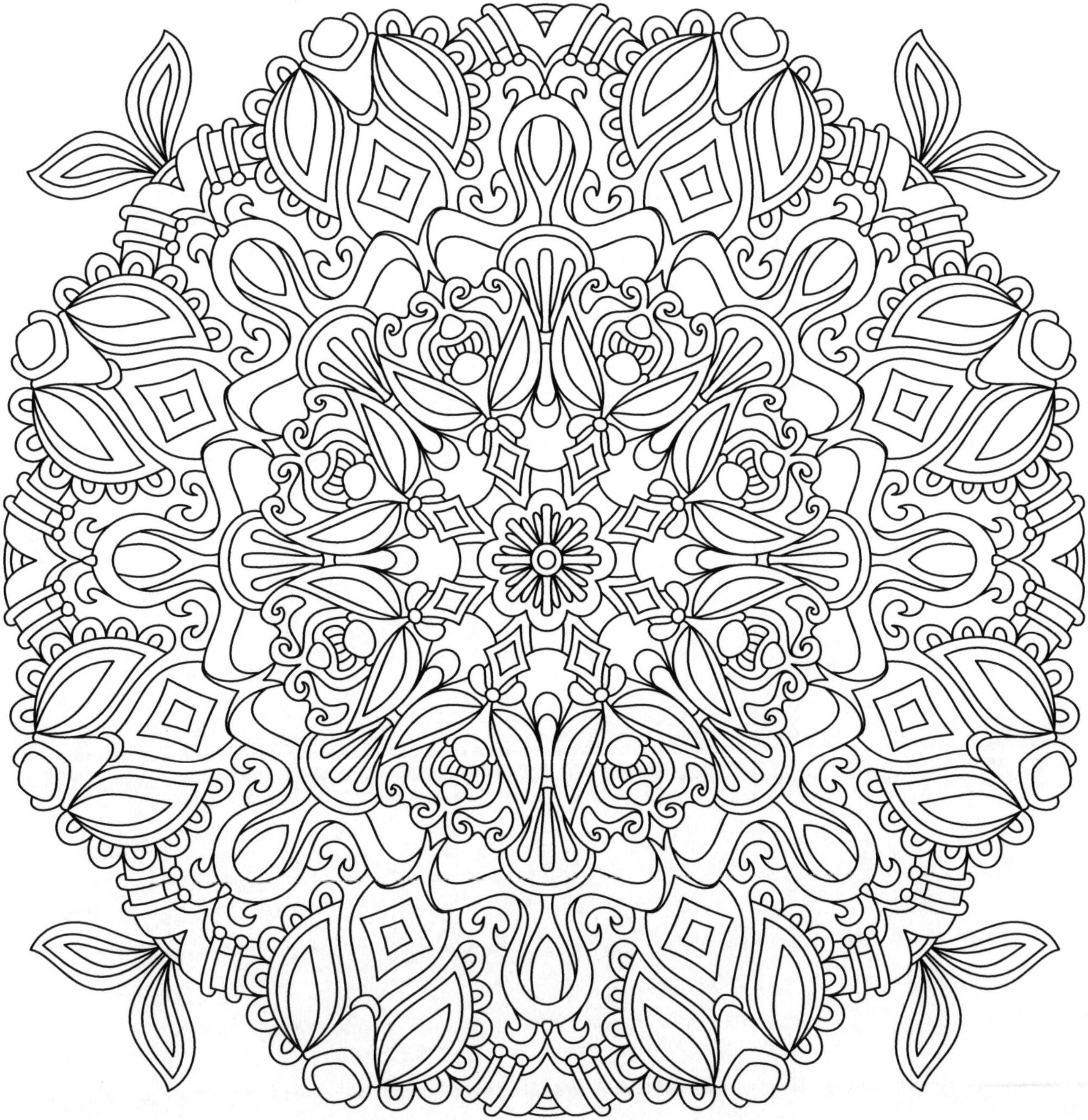

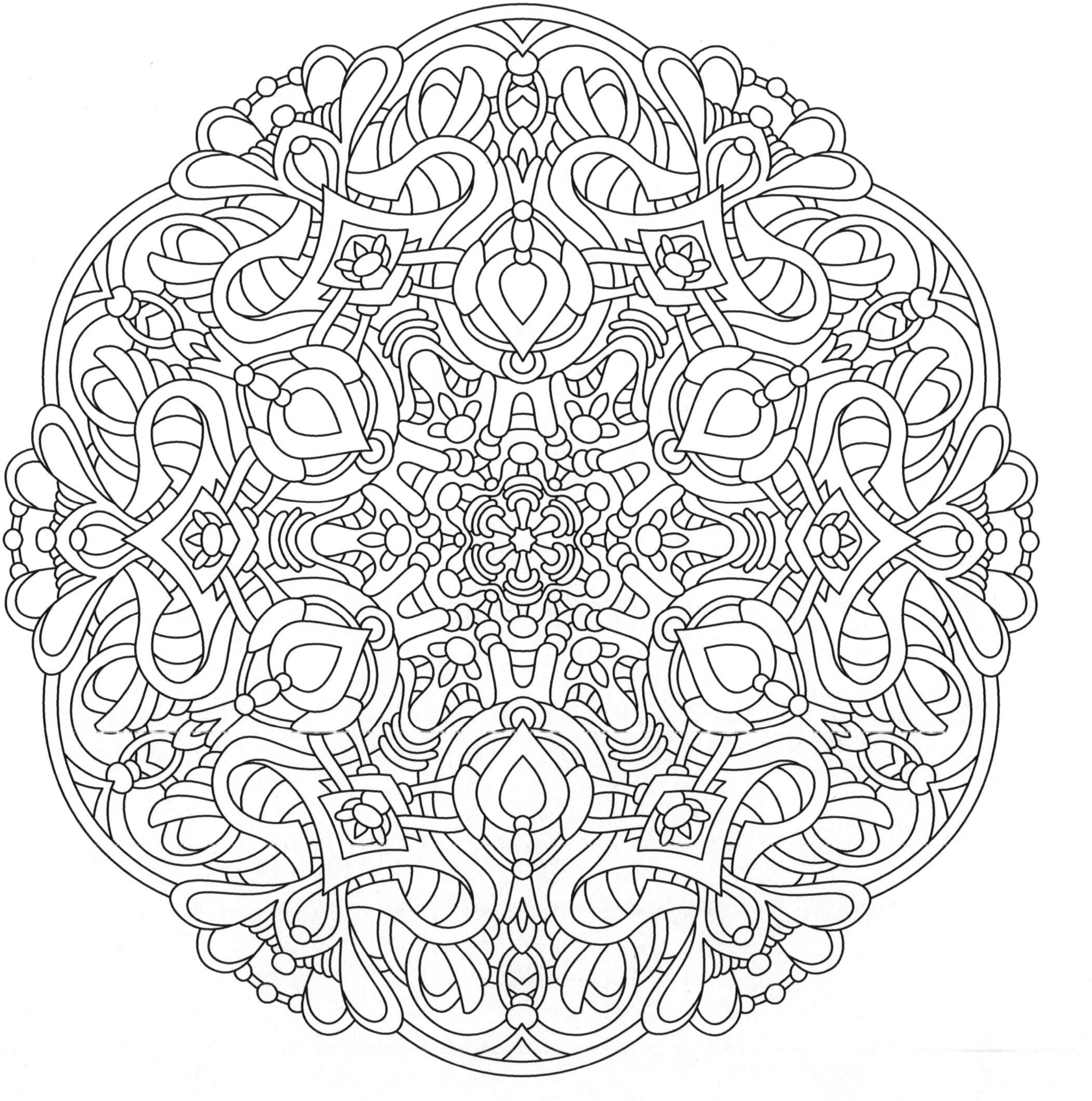

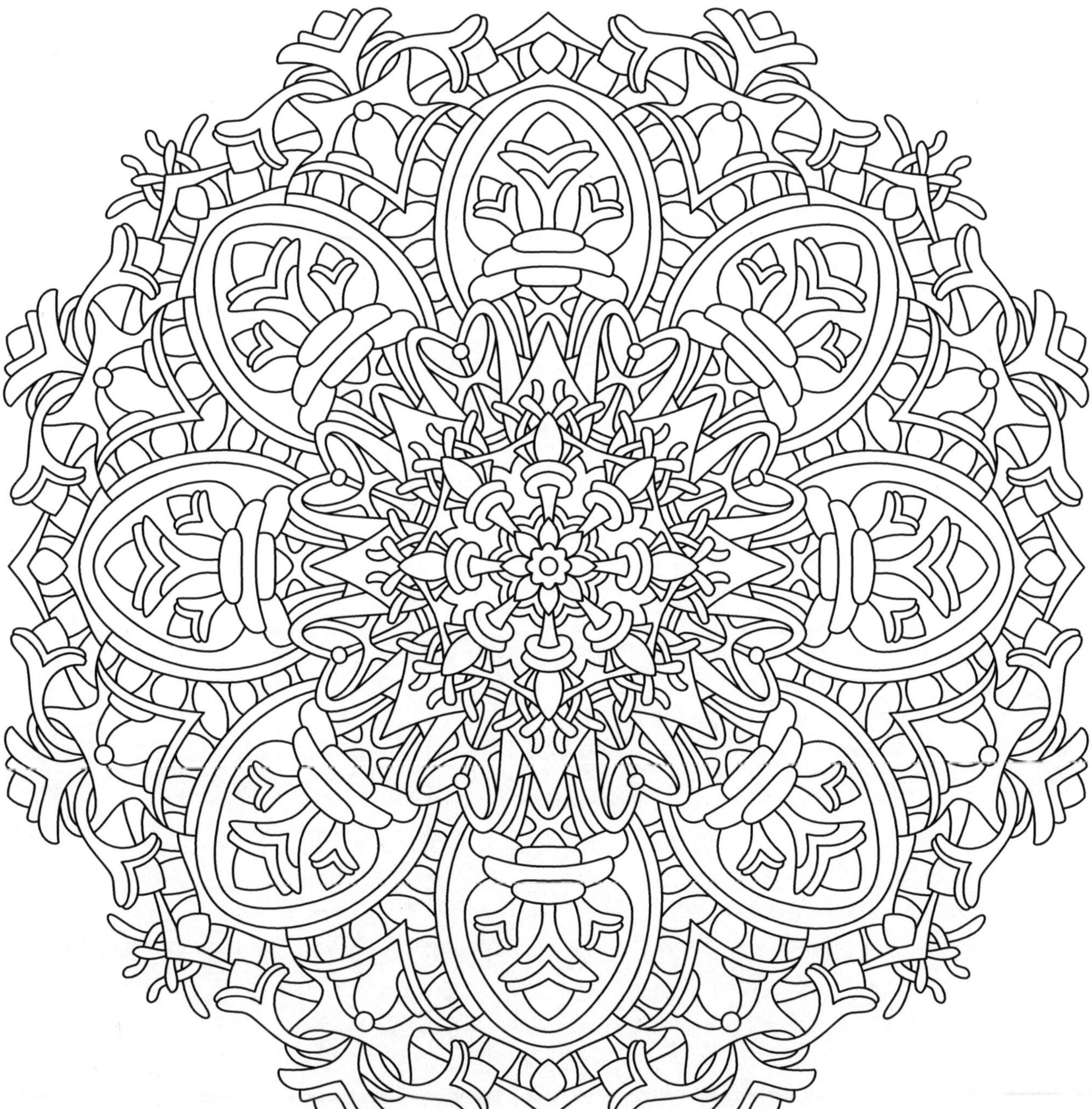

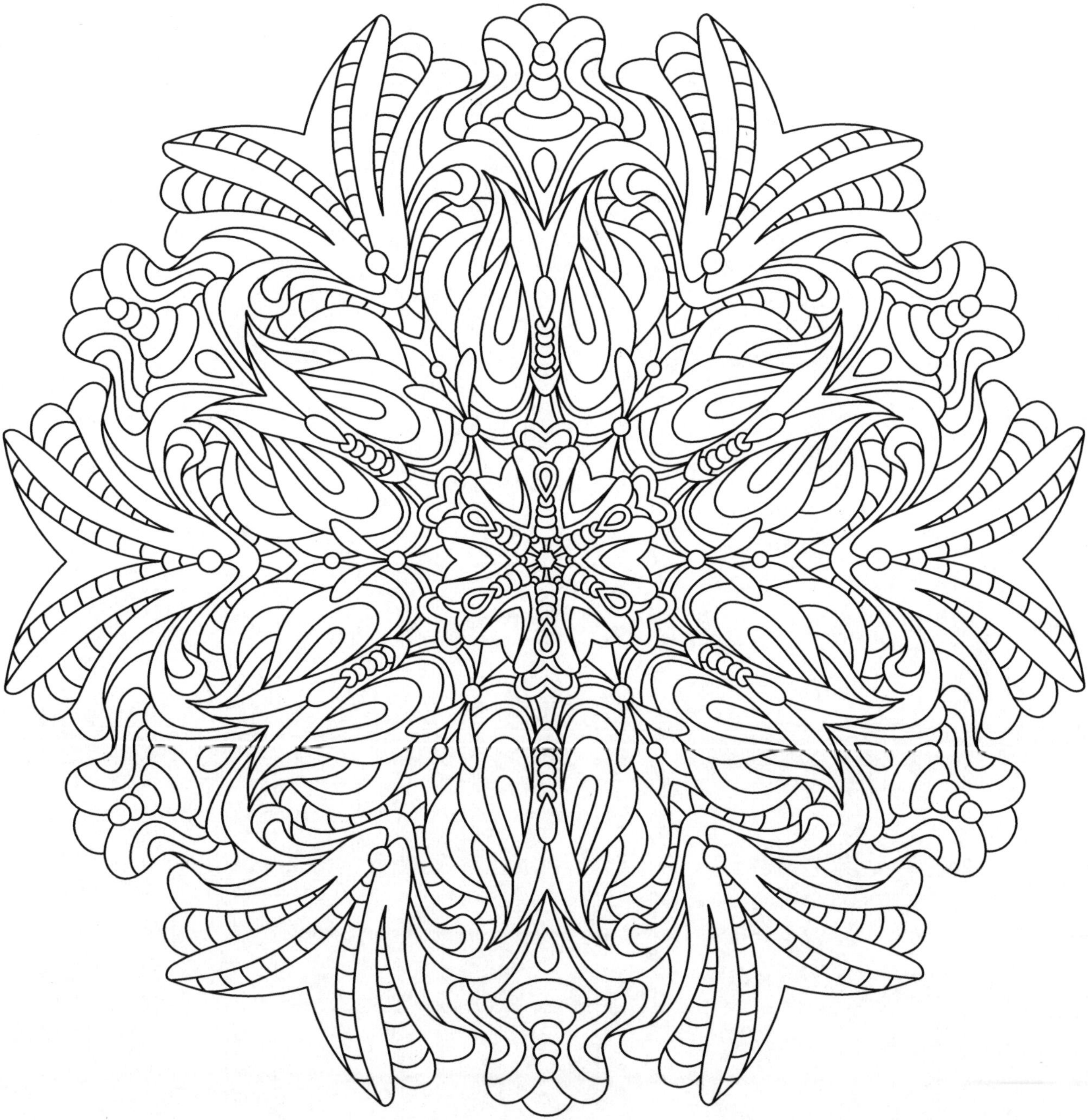

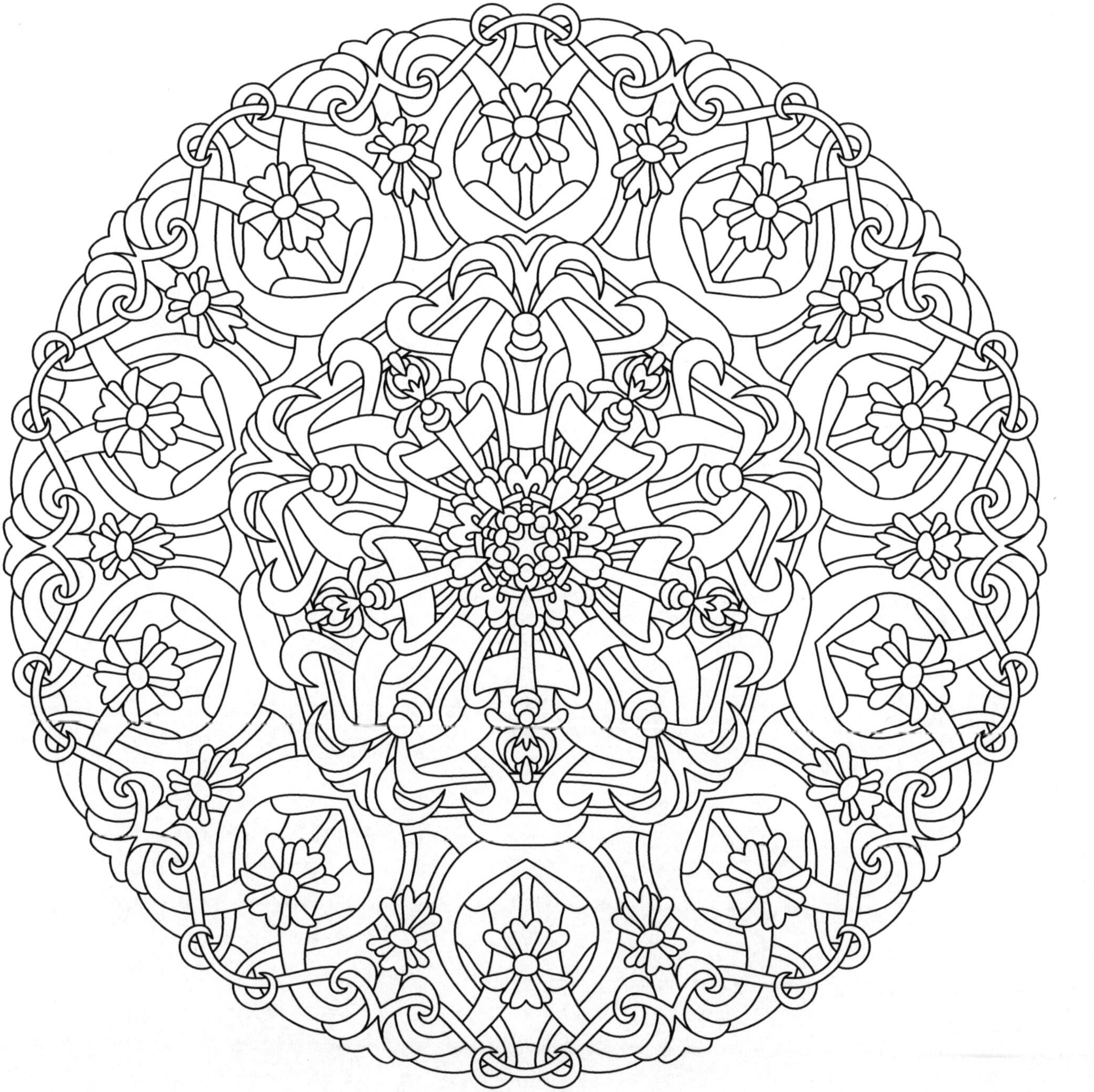

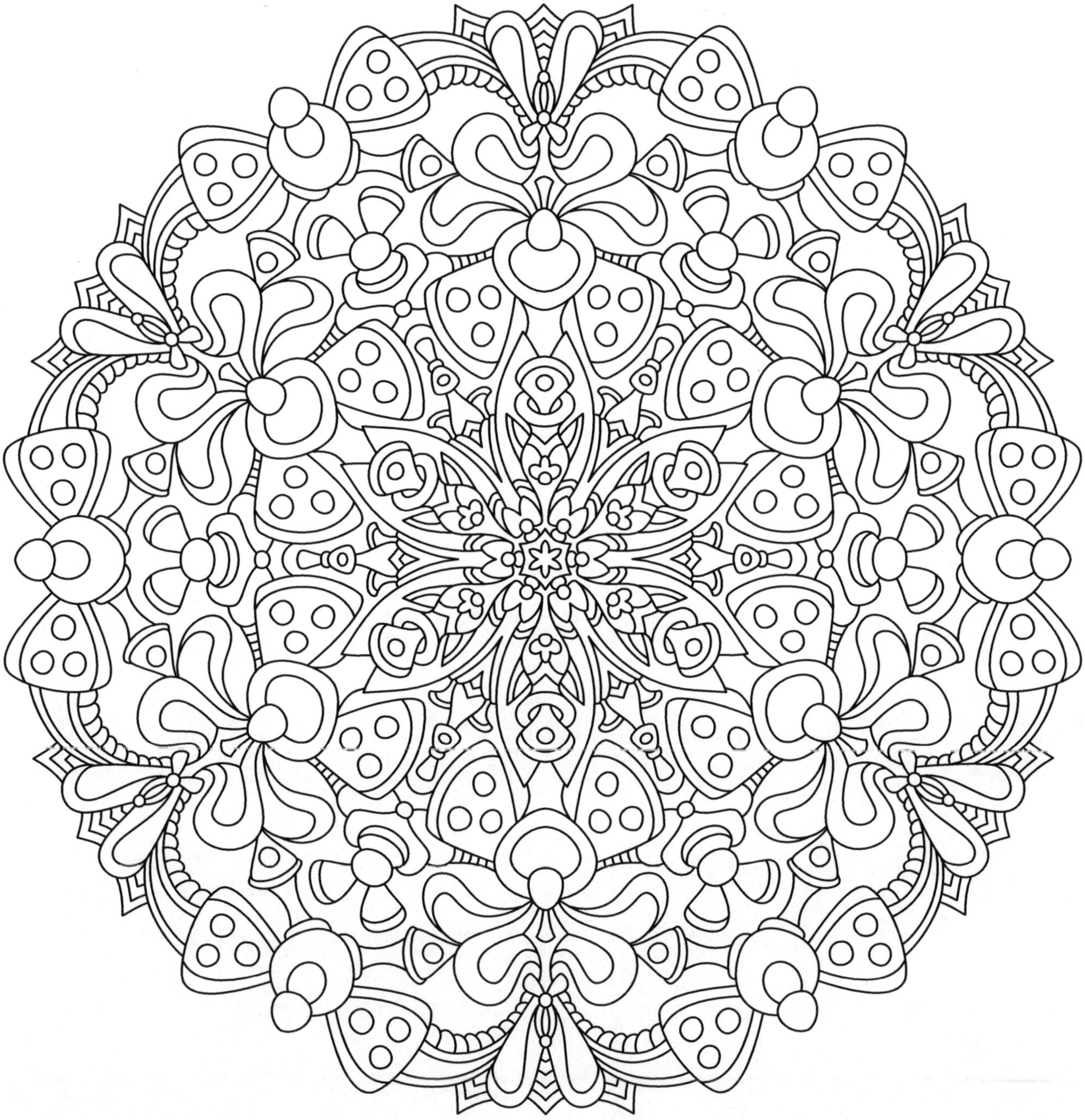

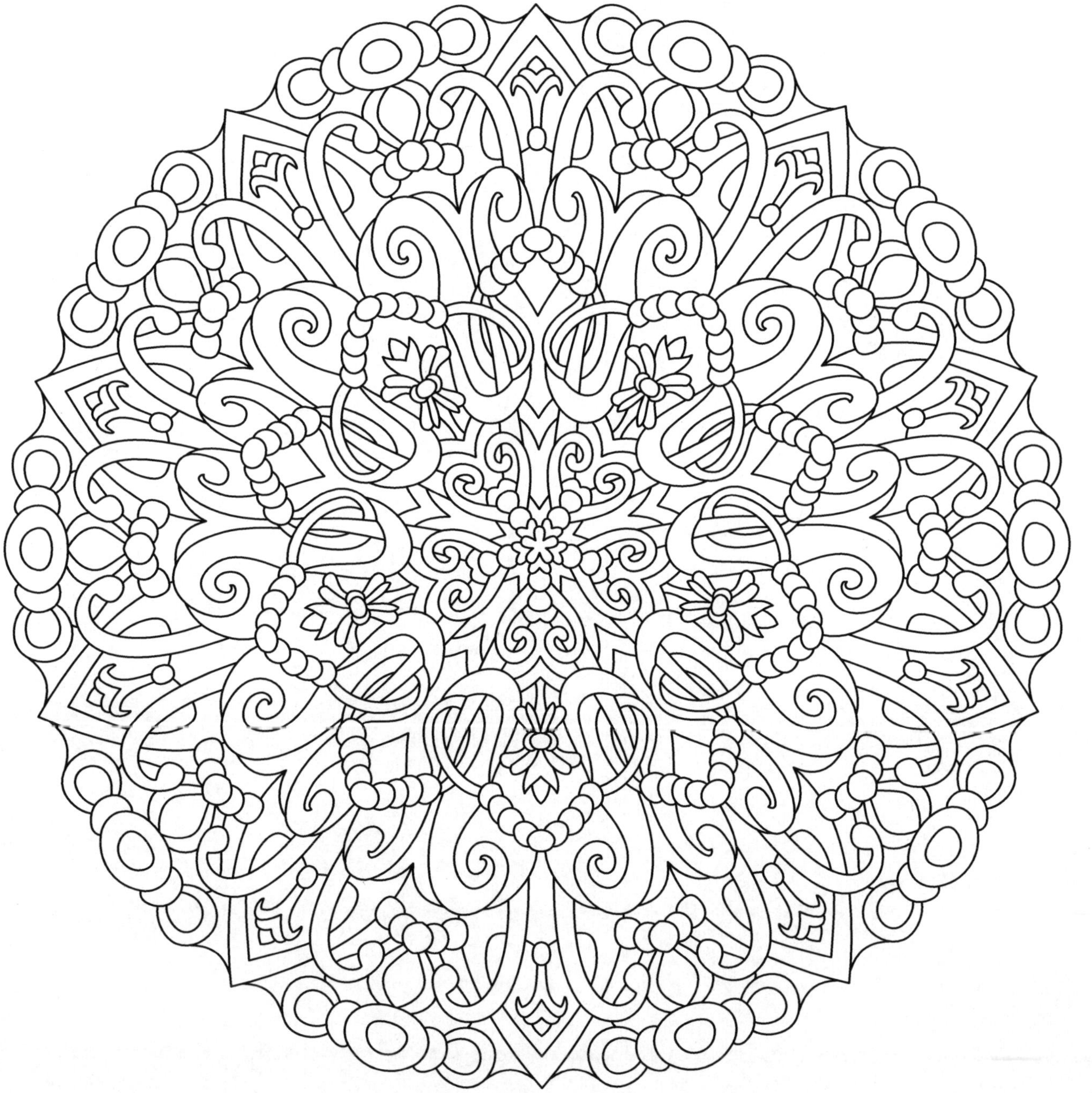

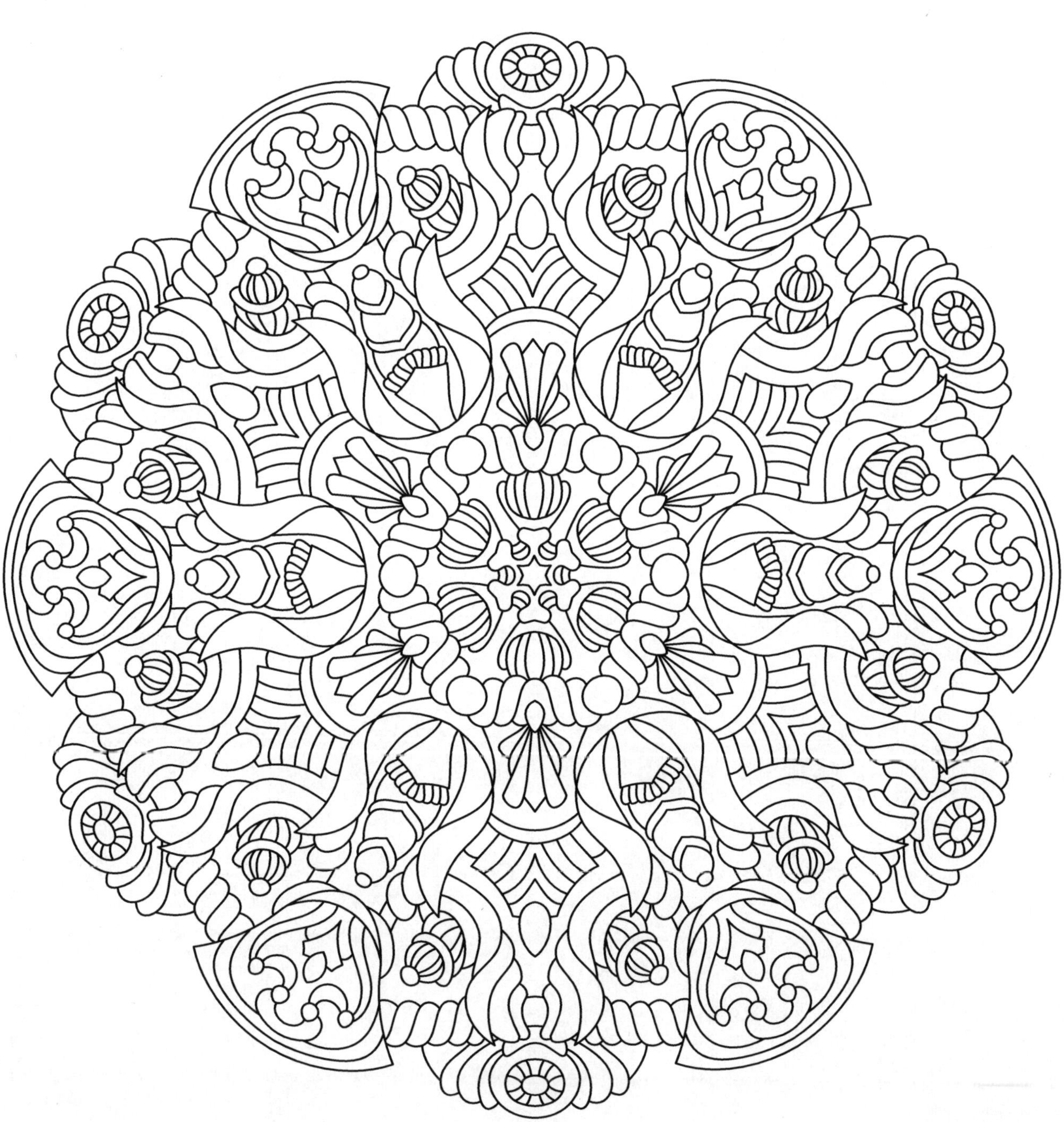

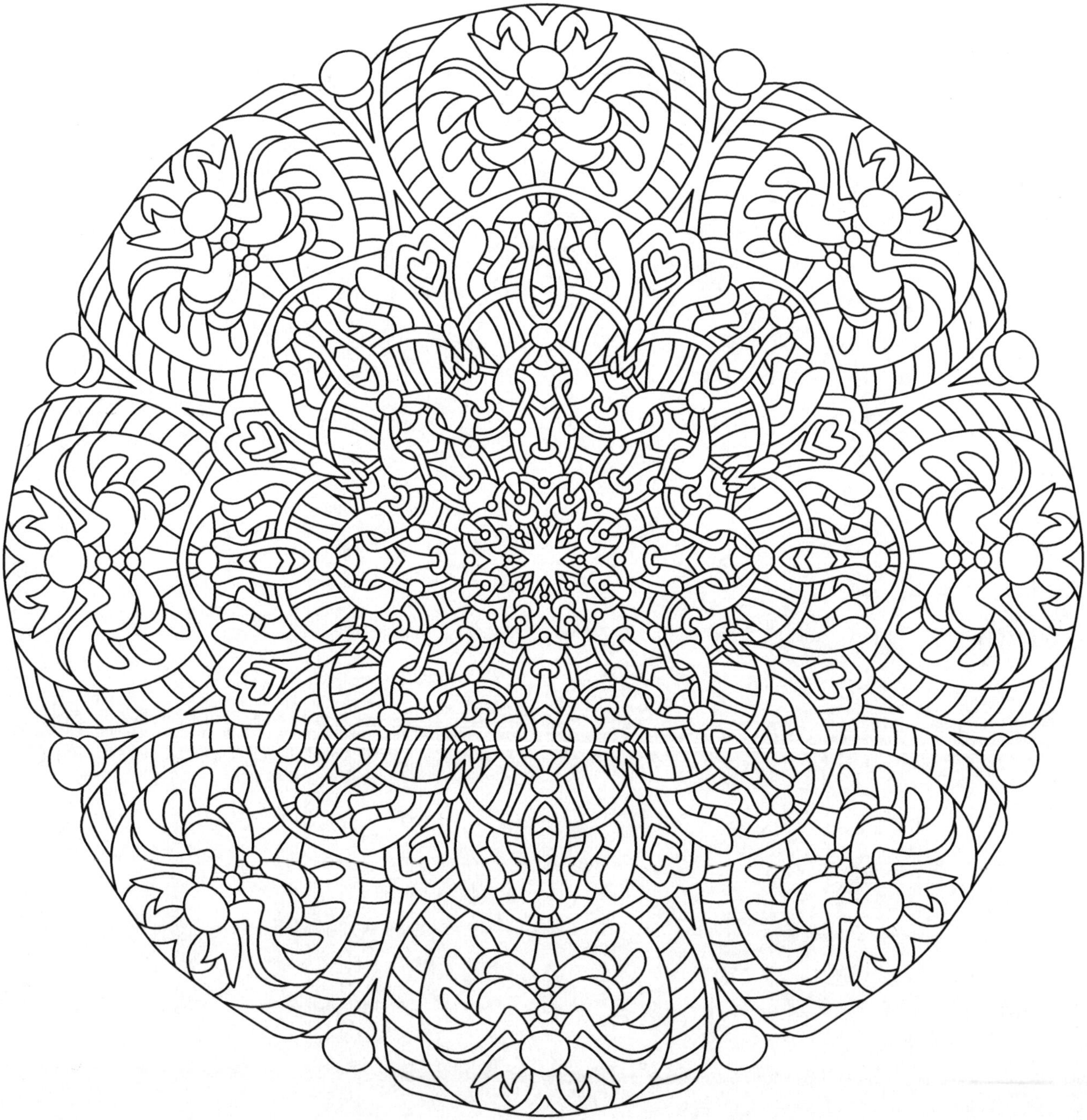

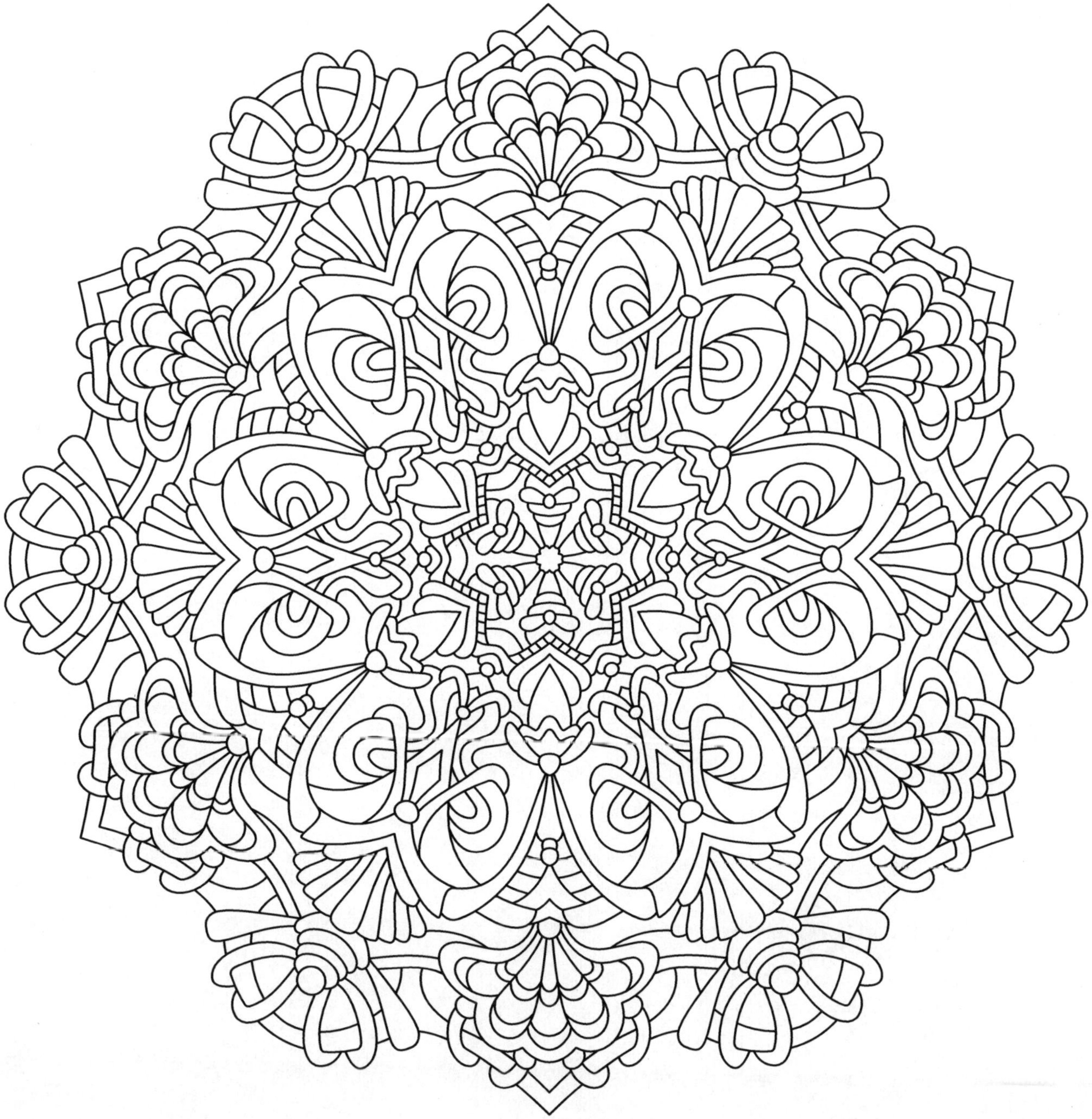

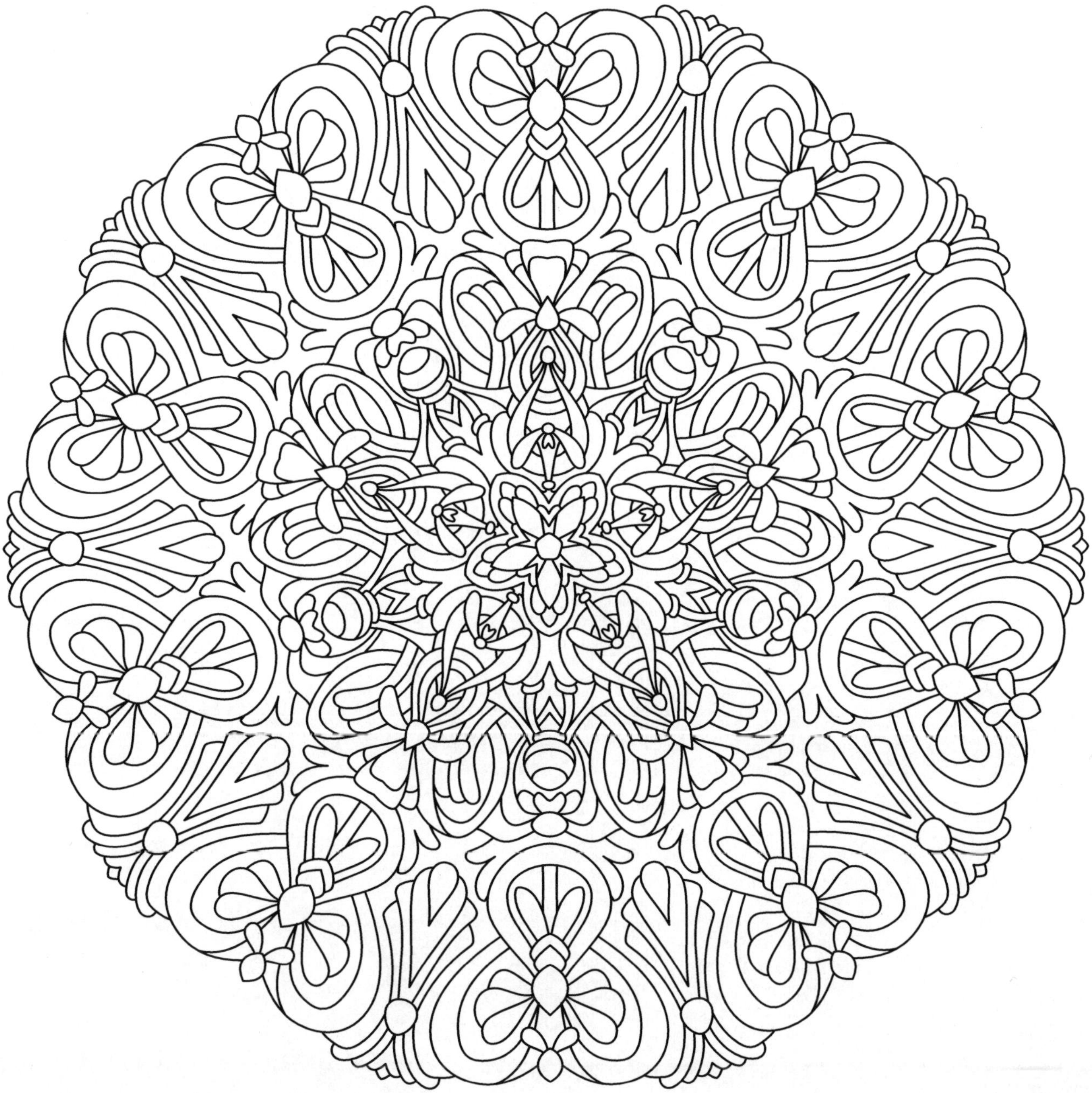

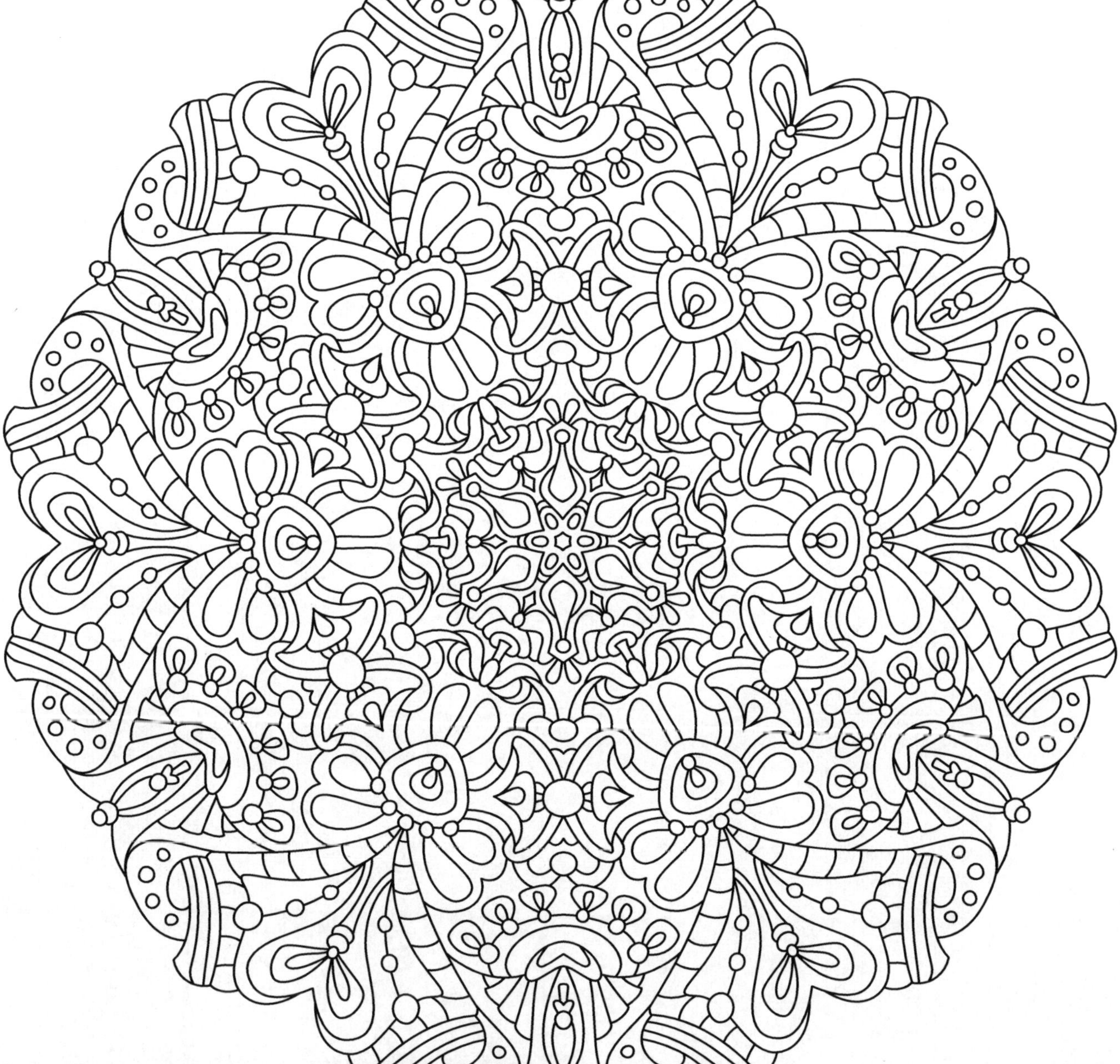

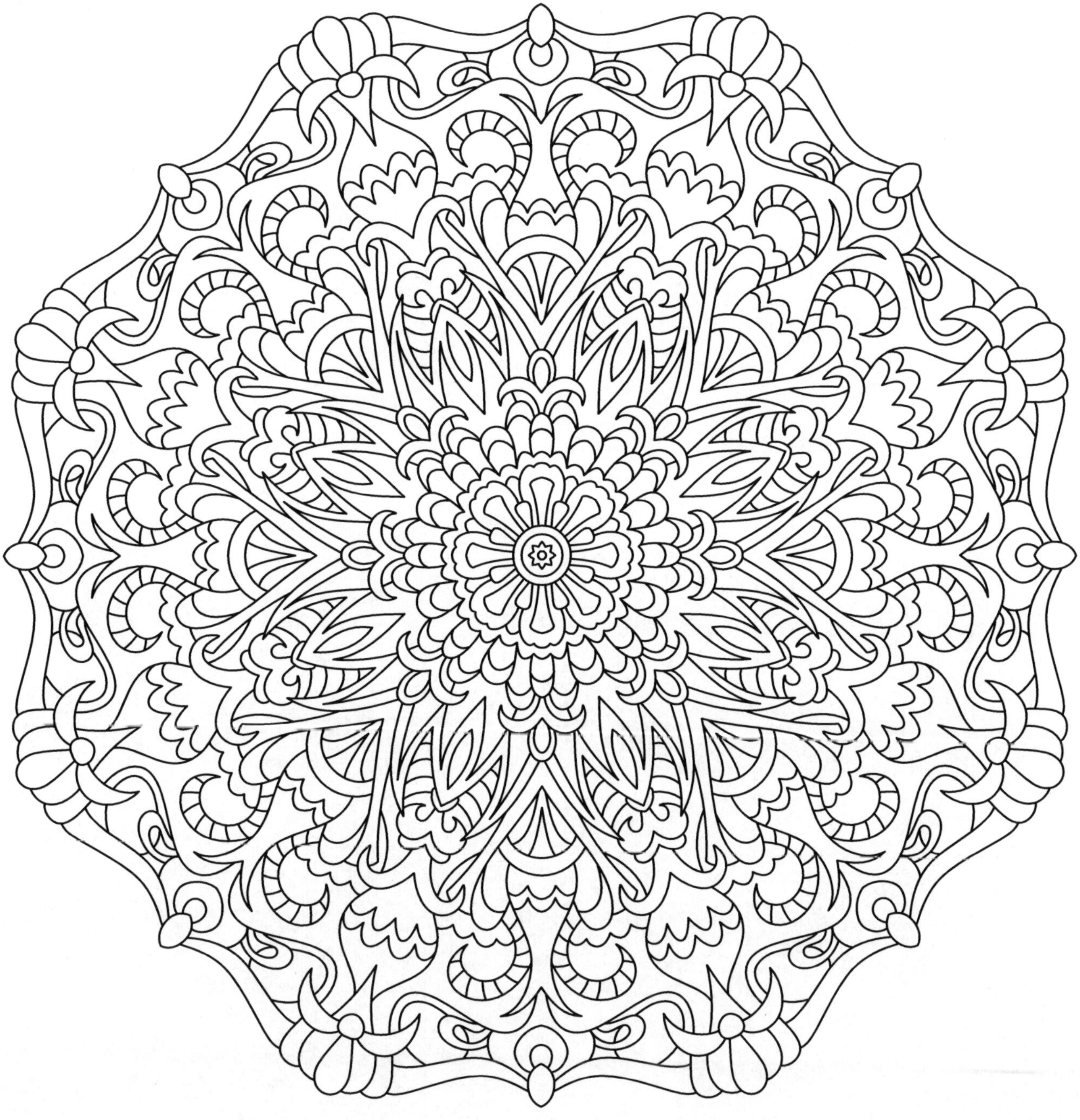

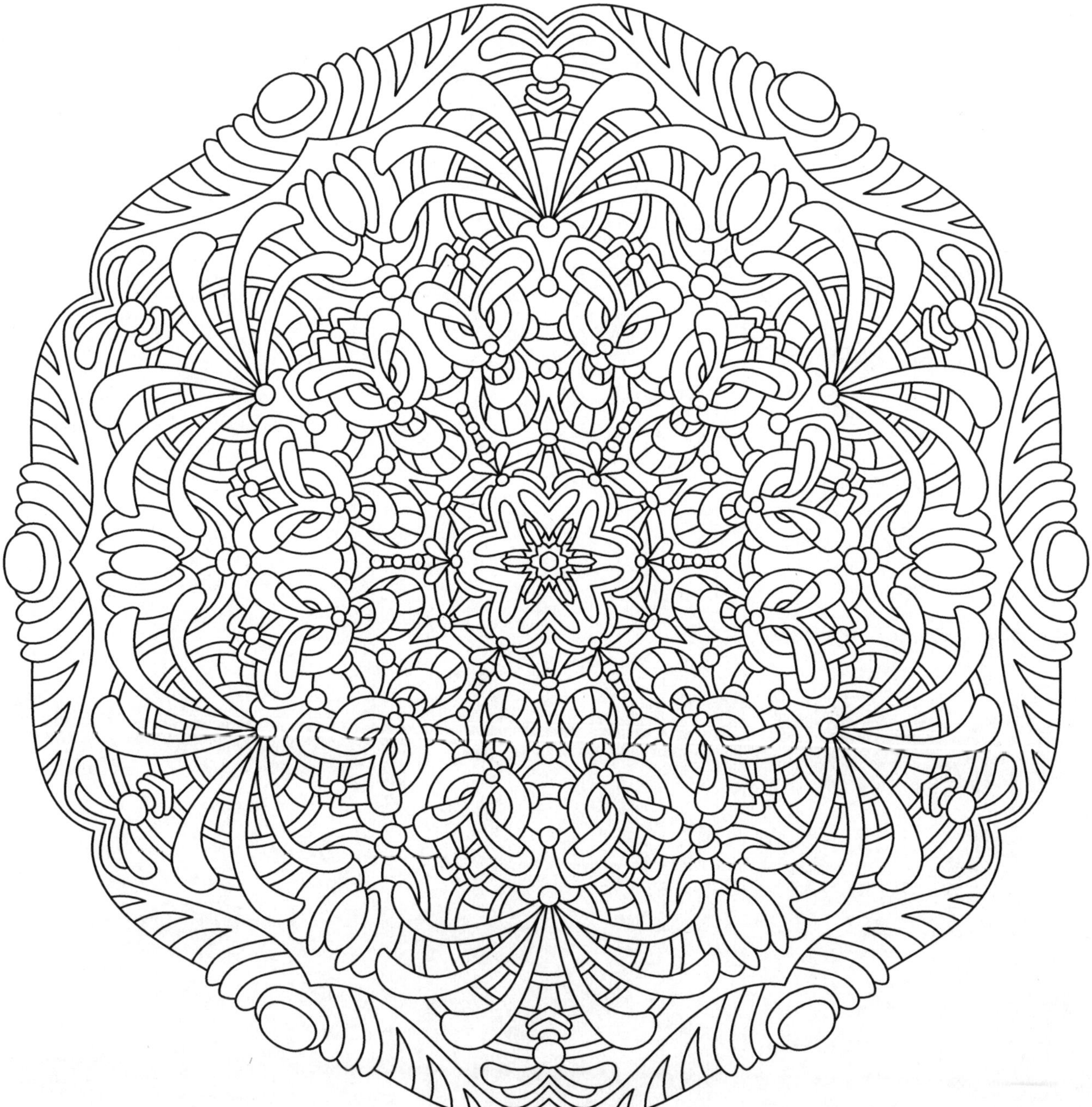

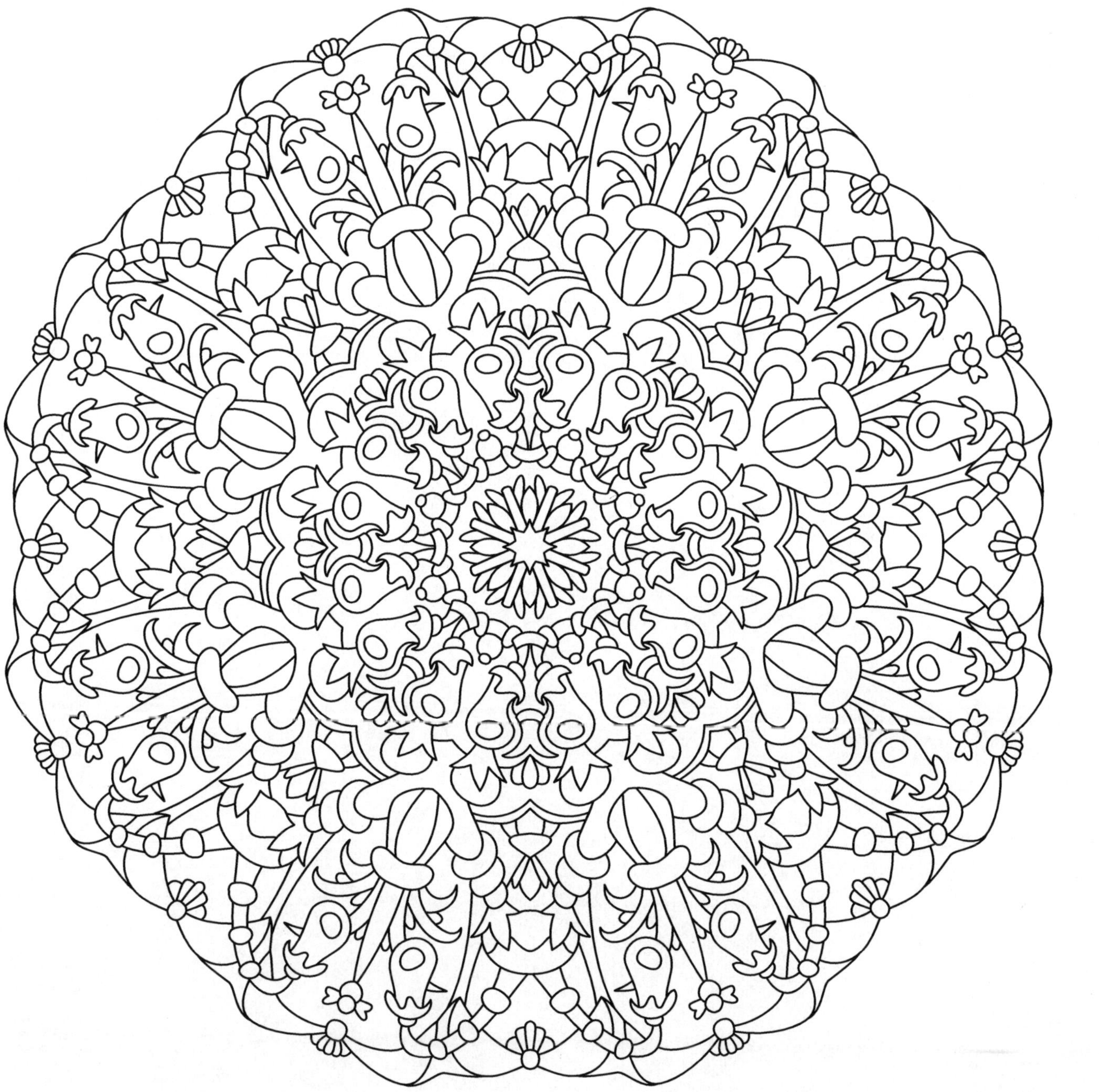

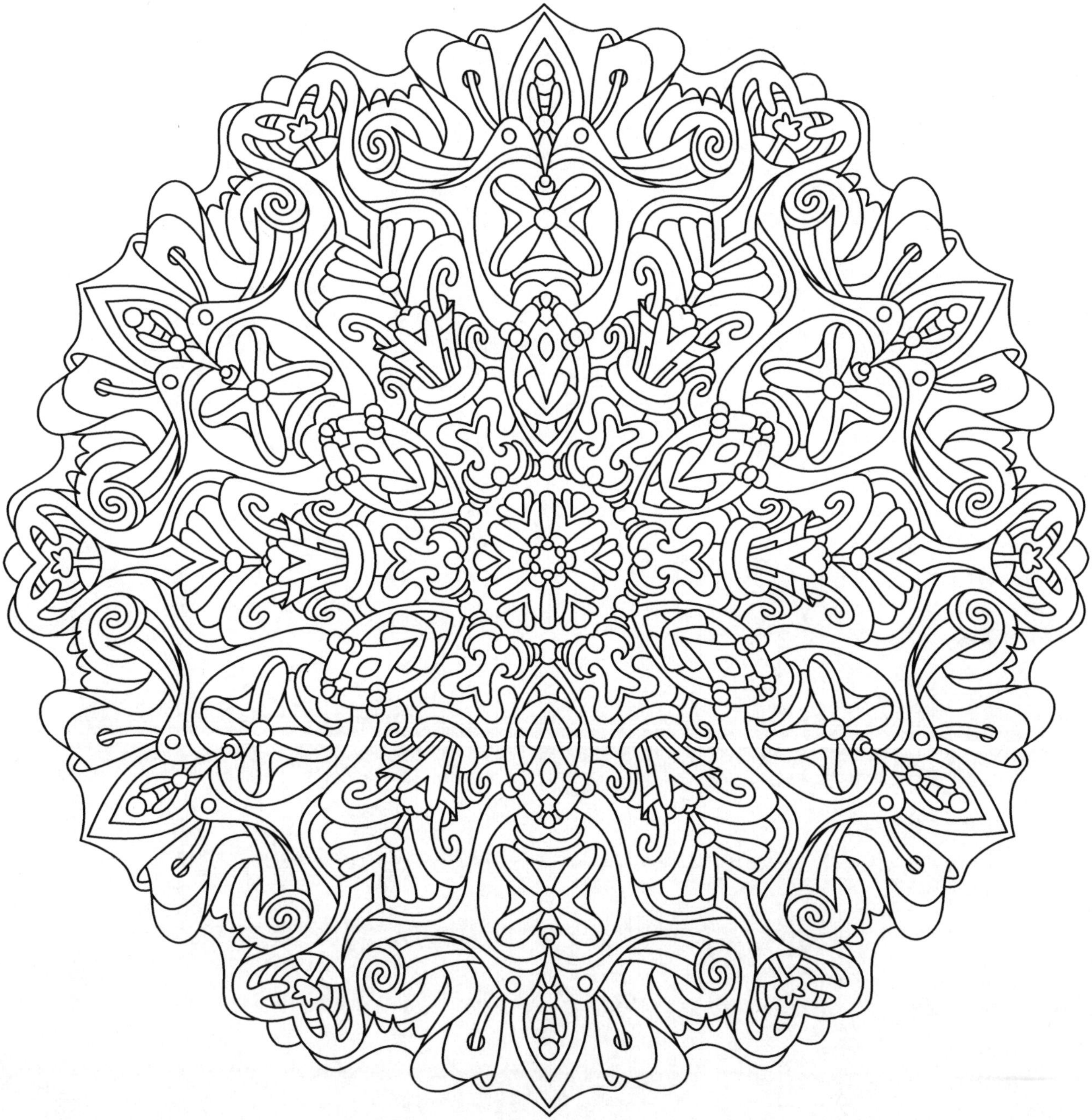

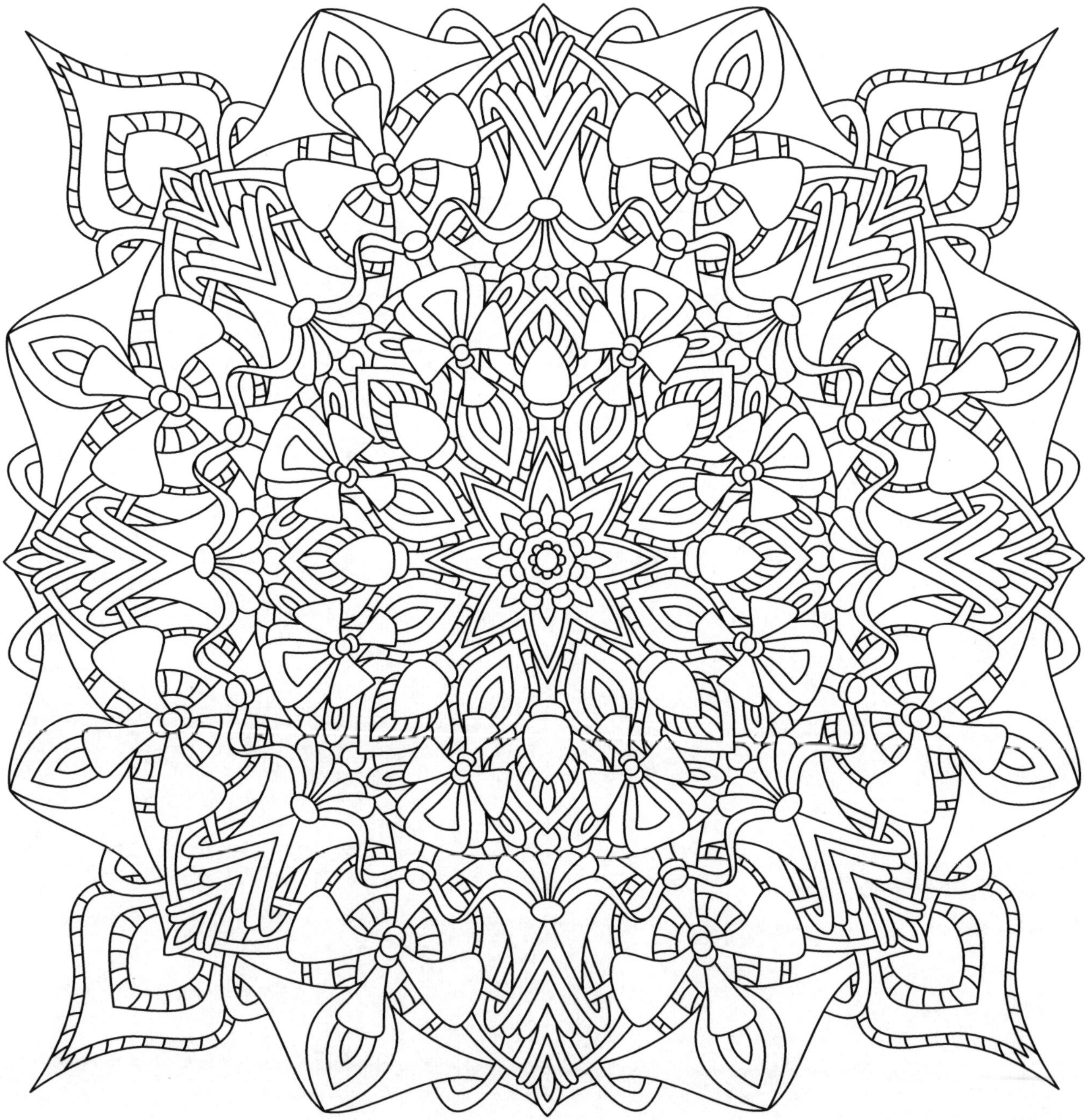

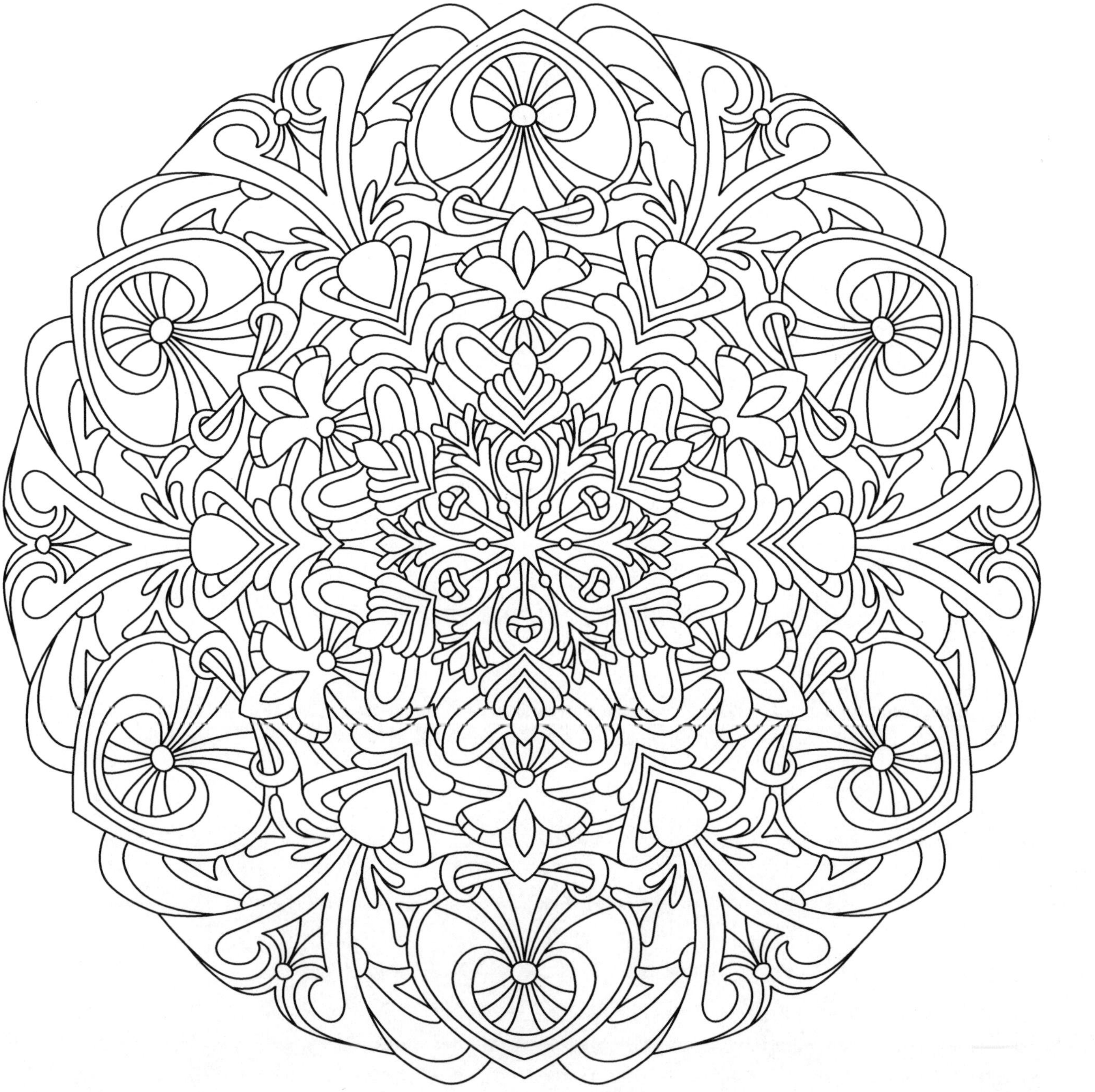

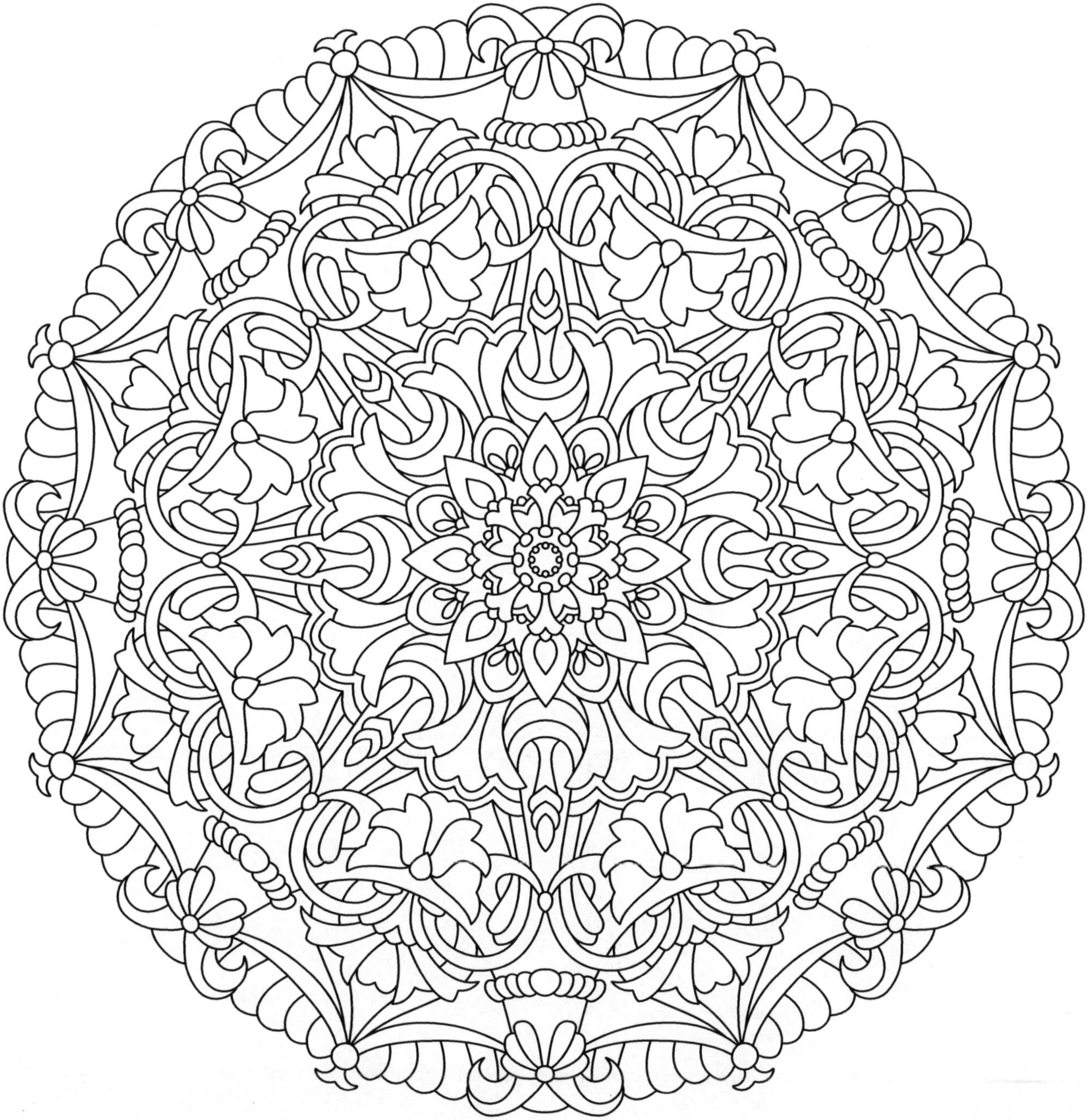

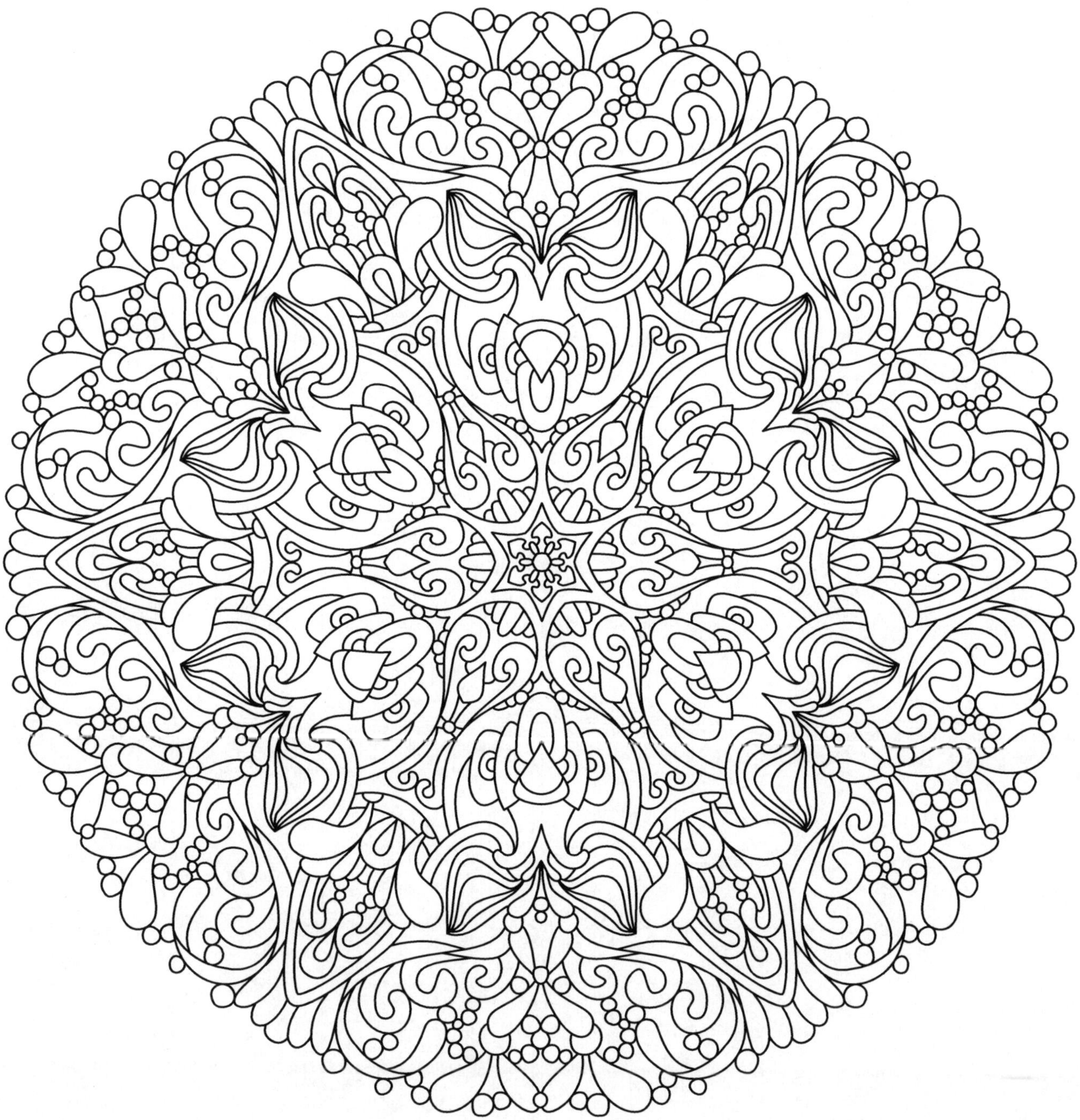

Visit Angie's website
for special web exclusives for colorists.

www.AngieGrace.com

Made in the USA
Columbia, SC
15 November 2024

46633414R00057